# CAREERS

# USING ENGLISH

David Roberts and Margaret Clewett

**KOGAN
PAGE**

The authors wish to thank all those who kindly contributed case studies for inclusion in this book. We are also grateful to Nicola Stephens at Kogan Page for her forbearance, and to Fiona, Joe and Madeleine for theirs.

First published in 1997

Kogan Page Limited
120 Pentonville Road
London N1 9JN

---

**British Library Cataloguing in Publication Data**

A CIP record for this book is available from the British Library.

ISBN 0 7494 2407 9

---

Typeset by Northern Phototypesetting Co Ltd, Bolton
Printed and bound in Great Britain by
Clays Ltd, St Ives plc

# Contents

# 1 Introduction: English and the world of work

## Is a career using English for You?

Are you interested in a subject which

- ☐ allows you to keep open a wide range of career options?
- ☐ can lead to work in advertising, publishing, marketing, journalism, information management, teaching and many other areas?
- ☐ gives you time to think about an equally wide range of personal, cultural and historical issues?
- ☐ teaches the key skills of careful reading, argument, synthesis, communication and personal organisation?
- ☐ encourages personal attributes consistently valued by employers?
- ☐ offers an excellent grounding for further study or training?
- ☐ can be approached by a variety of theoretical methods?
- ☐ encourages a more personal relationship between the student and the subject?
- ☐ enjoys a long-standing and respected base in higher education?

and, above all, one which

- ☐ rewards study with pleasure?

If your answers were mostly 'yes', then read on.

It is a little over one hundred years since English as an academic subject was established in the United Kingdom. There are arguments about why it developed: some point to its relationship to imperial conceptions of culture, others to the way English initially attracted groups of people who before had been denied access to mainstream academic study. Debate about the very nature and limits of the subject continues.

Two things, however, have never been in doubt: the popularity of English among students, and – teaching apart – its lack of any obvious relationship to the needs of the employment market. It is likely that those two facts are related, and certain that their relationship is, for some observers of the educational scene, infuriating. Large numbers of people are drawn to English because it offers intellectual freedom, the chance to pursue 'universal' questions through the pleasurable activity of reading imaginative fiction. It does not tie the student to a particular perspective on employment or, indeed, on life in general. Perhaps, some will say, it should. A disparaging view of the subject (which many of us have encountered in the form of the question, 'What's the use of doing that, then?') holds that English does not prepare students for the harsh realities of the work-place. By turning a hobby into a full-time occupation, and by inviting an endlessly questioning approach to received opinion, it simply fails to inculcate the necessary discipline – or so the argument goes. As one observer of the Higher Education scene has recently put it, 'developing understanding is inherently subversive' (from Ronald Barnett, *The Limits of Competence: Knowledge, Higher Education and Society*, Open University Press, 1994, p 105).

If this were the whole truth, you might expect people with English qualifications to do less well in the employment market than they actually do. In fact, English graduates in particular are remarkably adept at getting good jobs, and in an unexpectedly wide range of careers. What is the explanation? Do English students learn 'transferable skills' without always knowing it, or do they simply tend to demonstrate appealing personal qualities which may or may not have been enhanced by their studies? A recent report argues that all graduates benefit from Higher Education in the jobs market for the latter reason; in other words, a degree helps to get you a job but not to do it (see the preliminary DfEE report by Paul Richardson *et al.* in the *Bookseller*, vol 27, October 1995, pp.18–19). If that is true, it is not necessarily very helpful to anyone thinking about a career or looking for a job, since personal qualities are rather harder to develop than specific skills. For the purposes of this book, therefore, it will be assumed that English does – contrary to popular opinion – instil a number of skills which are marketable, adaptable and sophisticated, and the fact that English graduates end up in so many different types of employment is a sign of the subject's vitality and rigour.

Here are the chief conclusions of a recent report on graduate employment, *What Do Graduates Do?* (UCAS/CSU, 1997).

◆ English graduates enter a very wide range of career areas.
◆ A large percentage go on to further study, both academic and vocational.
◆ Media-related careers feature at a small but significant level.

Taken together, these indicate:

a) the diversity of employment situations in which former English students succeed;
b) the adaptability of English graduates not only to work but to further study, both in and beyond higher education;
c) the prominence, notwithstanding, of attractive areas like the media which are traditionally associated with the subject.

The key word here is *adaptability*. You won't need reminding that that has also become the key word for approaching employment towards and after the millennium. This book contains a number of case studies, the careers to date of people like you. They are all people who, through a determination to succeed, have adapted themselves intelligently to their circumstances: people who have thought laterally, pursuing the less obvious routes to their chosen destinations and refusing to be downcast by initial failure. Very few people enjoy an unbroken path to success: for most it is a question of finding the right stepping-stones and being prepared to take the occasional move backwards or sideways to reach the ultimate goal.

Romantic dreams surround the student of English: writing, the theatre, all kinds of glamorous careers seem to beckon. The reality is that most students of the subject learn to apply their many skills in a variety of settings. This book is intended for the many.

## Breakdown of first destinations

It is important to stress the 'first' in 'first destinations', because students of English very often move from one employment sector to another. This part of the book shows the variety of starting points.

*What Do Graduates Do?* charted the first destinations of over 2000 1995 UK English graduates, and came up with these results:

**Table 1.1** *First destinations*

|                                                        | Per cent |
|--------------------------------------------------------|----------|
| In UK employment                                       | 46.5     |
| In overseas employment                                 | 3.2      |
| Further academic study (including teacher training)    | 30.4     |
| Other training                                         | 1.5      |
| Training or study overseas                             | 0.6      |
| Not available for employment, study or training        | 5.7      |
| Believed unemployed                                    | 10.2     |

It is encouraging to note that the proportion entering full-time employment and the proportion undertaking further study or training are relatively high, while the unemployment rate is below the average for all graduates.

Now look at the *kinds of work* undertaken by graduates covered by the same survey.

**Table 1.2** *Kinds of work*

|  | Per cent |
| --- | --- |
| Administration and management | 18.7 |
| Teaching | 2.7 |
| Business/financial | 3.2 |
| Social work | 1.4 |
| Literary/artistic/sports | 8.0 |
| Other professional/technical occupations | 5.8 |
| Clerical and secretarial | 27.5 |
| Personal/protective service occupations | 10.0 |
| Sales/marketing/buying | 15.9 |
| Other occupations | 6.8 |

The organisations included in these figures include banks, bakeries, publishers, advertising agents, accountants, financial analysts, bookshops, newspapers, the government, supermarkets, and many others. There are some big names here – the BBC, Debenhams, Thomson Newspapers, Zeneca, Virgin Megastores, P & O, The Prince's Trust, Sainsbury's, National Opinion Poll, Waterstone's – as well as a wide range of smaller, local employers. In addition, students surveyed had gone on to complete certificate, diploma or master's level qualifications in (among others) nursing, journalism, publishing, teaching, acting, personnel management, social work and law.

You can read more about the diversity of destinations for English graduates in the later chapters of this book. Now it is time to focus on the reasons why English proves such an adaptable subject.

Please note that the Association of Graduate Careers Advisory Services is referred to as AGCAS throughout the book.

# 2 The skills you learn through studying English

It will help to bear in mind that employers classically value three qualities above everything else: problem-solving, creativity, social skills.

These are notoriously difficult to define, and they turn out to mean quite different things depending on what subject or employment situation you are talking about. Some employers will talk not of 'social' but of 'communication' skills; for 'creativity' others will substitute 'self-reliance' or 'flexibility'; for 'problem-solving' you could read simply 'planning and organisation'. Even the greatest educational buzz term of our time – 'learning how to learn' – is fraught with controversy. For an employer it may signify an ability to meet new practical or methodological challenges whenever they arise, an ability born of a set of fundamental competences in communication, reasoning, numeracy, information technology and so on. For an academic, however, learning how to learn may simply be an ethical precondition for academic study, an acceptance of the provisional nature of all knowledge. It does not take much to see that the two definitions are hard to square.

Just because the key terms are hard to define, however, does not mean that they signify nothing. The aim of this chapter is to show just how many skills the study of English encourages, and how marketable those skills demonstrably are in the employment scene. The intention is not to suggest that by studying English you are locking yourself into a course in competences for employment – perish the thought! What is proposed is that the very open-endedness of the subject encourages the development of those broader, hard-to-define attributes which employers appear to want. There are individual, 'transferable' skills in English which you can bring to your career, but there are also habits of mind which inform life and career alike, consciously or otherwise. What then are those skills and habits?

## Critical thinking

English students are expected to think for themselves. This takes several forms:

◆ close reading of texts;
◆ putting texts and arguments in their context, whether critical, historical or theoretical;
◆ interrogating primary evidence;
◆ uncovering the assumptions behind a given statement;
◆ debating received views on the basis of their explicit or implicit arguments;
◆ summarising.

Surveys indicate that English graduates view these skills as particularly valuable in their chosen jobs.

## Interpersonal skills

English students tend to be articulate and confident when compared to their peers in other subjects. As you may already have noticed, there are not so many absolute rights and wrongs in English as there are, say, in biology: there is always room for interpretation and argument. This means that English students are encouraged from the start to share ideas and develop them constructively with other people. In this subject, you learn to *listen* by

◆ finding out what other people have to say;
◆ drawing them into discussion;
◆ showing that you understand and are interested;
◆ finding the right time to question or take issue;

and you learn to *discuss* by:

- ◆ proposing ideas;
- ◆ making them sound appealing;
- ◆ knowing when to stop;
- ◆ taking account of opposing views;
- ◆ reflecting on your own position.

You may be assessed formally on your ability to do these things, but even if you are not, it pays to work at them.

## Communication

We have looked at oral communication skills. Another reason why English specialists do well in the employment market is that they learn to write accurately in a variety of formats: essays, reports, summaries, commentaries, and so on. Acquiring knowledge of the generic characteristics of a given form of writing is crucial to successful communication. The more practice you get at writing, the more adaptable your skills become.

## Organisational skills

All students have to organise their time effectively in order to make personal ambitions and learning styles conform to a common structure of classes and assessment deadlines. What is different in English is that a great deal of time is taken up by what can be an open-ended and distractingly enjoyable activity: reading the primary texts. Because this represents such a problem of time management, English students may become more ingenious in devising solutions to help them through. They learn to manage the sheer quantity of primary reading by:

- ◆ identifying structural features of texts which enable them to be comprehended more swiftly;

◆ supplying critical, historical or theoretical contexts to provide a framework of understanding;

◆ sharing their experience of the primary texts with other students.

Such strategies often transfer well to the work-place.

## Information gathering and analysis

Academic study is nothing if not an exercise in information retrieval, and today there is an increasing emphasis on the individual student's responsibility for doing just that. The basic tools of English studies are the primary texts and the critical reading associated with them, but these are just a small part of the panoply of information sources which you may use during your course: whether bound, on-line, or on CD-ROM, library catalogues, reference books, concordances or annotated bibliographies, all entail versatility and a sense of initiative in the user. More than that, they demand a strictly evaluative approach to the information retrieved. English has been defined as a science of interpretation whose main weapon is suspicion, and its students learn to bring to all sources of information a sense that something better may be found elsewhere.

Now spend some time reflecting on which of the skills and habits listed above you have brought to your English studies so far, and which ones you need to work at. Give some thought, too, to the way in which any work or leisure experience you may have had has contributed to them. This is essential preparation for the task of marketing yourself to employers.

Chapters 3–12 introduce you to ten employment areas in which people with English qualifications have been successful. For each area there are job descriptions, background information, lists of necessary attributes, tips for getting in, case studies, useful addresses and further sources of information. As you read, try to map each career option on to your understanding of your own strengths, weaknesses, inclinations and ambitions. Talk to friends and family about their sense of your suitability for this or that career. Pay particular attention to the tips for getting in, and, if you are sufficiently interested in one career, sketch out a possible plan of action which would get you moving towards it. When you read a case study, don't be put off too soon by the thought that 'that isn't me', because the person it is about probably thought the same a few years ago!

When you apply for a job, you'll have to prove that you're equipped for it. For advice about writing up your English skills and qualifications on a CV or application form, consult the following:

## Further reading

There are lots of useful books on marketing yourself:

Chris Phillips's *Making Wizard Applications* (Just the Job Handbooks); *The Creative Job Search*, published by the University of Warwick Careers Service, and *How to Write a Curriculum Vitae*, published by the Career Service of the University of London; Sue O'Rourke's *The Jobseeker's Guide to Success* (Pentland Press); Steve Morris and Graham Willcocks's *Successful CVs in a Week* (Headway – Hodder and Stoughton); not forgetting the AGCAS booklet, *Applications and Interviews*.

# 3 Advertising

Advertising is an attractive but competitive profession. It is also an industry where huge amounts of money are spent every year: in 1995, £10,959 million was spent on advertising in the UK. Seventy-five percent of this sum went into TV, radio, cinema, billboard, press and mailshot advertising, the remainder on recruitment, professional and small ads. With the diversification of the media, advertising has a dynamic future.

The biggest share is spent on advertising in the press: that is, in the 11 national dailies, 11 Sundays, 18 regional morning papers, 72 regional evening papers, seven regional Sundays, 473 local weeklies, 2100 special interest magazines and 4000 business and professional magazines, not to mention the hundreds of consumer magazines, free distribution and controlled circulation publications. When you add to this electronic and open-air advertising you begin to see that the scope of the industry is enormous. If you are interested in advertising as a career, spend some time looking at the range of styles and methods used in different media, and read the top tips for getting in on p 14.

The advertising industry covers three groups:

◆ *users* (the companies who advertise products or services);
◆ *makers* (the agencies who devise advertising strategy);
◆ *displayers* (the media organisations responsible for carrying advertisements).

Remember that it is not just agencies who devise strategy: users may have in-house advertising departments, while displayers have to show market awareness. Users may include companies, charities, local government and political parties. Whether you are a user, a maker or a displayer, the skills you need to advertise are essentially the same.

The working environment of advertising involves:

- ◆ a clear understanding of the market;
- ◆ strict deadlines;
- ◆ tight time schedules;
- ◆ unpredictable and often long hours (advertising is not a nine-to-five job!);
- ◆ a variety of tasks;
- ◆ team work;
- ◆ constant communication with clients and colleagues;
- ◆ sound numeracy;
- ◆ relative freedom from bureaucracy;
- ◆ generally pleasant surroundings.

It is this combination, together with the glamour and prestige associated with the industry, which attracts young people to it. But be warned: competition is stiff, and the work can be extremely pressurised.

## The jobs

The following examples are taken from the most specialised sector of advertising: the makers or agencies. This is because they tend to have the greatest range of functions, even though their total number of employees is relatively small (only about 20,000 nationwide). Getting into an advertising agency is very tough indeed, but this section will tell you about the kinds of work available in the sector at large.

### Account manager

The account manager is the main contact between the agency and the client, and will look after the business of two or three separate customers. S/he may be helped by account executives and report to the account director. Responsible for the administration and profitability of the account, s/he will pass on the client's wishes to the account team and promote the team's recommendations to the client. A lot of time is spent in situations requiring developed social and organisational skills: chairing meetings, making presentations, soothing nerves, and so on. Account managers generally start as account executives, and it is worth pointing out that half of account executives and executive trainees work in London. The rest are distributed in cities up and down the country.

## Account executive

It is up to the account executive to understand the client's market by, for example, scanning magazines, attending market research sessions, liaising with the client's own marketing department, and so on. S/he will also be in charge of the nuts and bolts arrangements of advertising: making sure that media space has been booked and keeping track of invoices. One slip here could lead to considerable embarrassment, to say the least!

## Account planner

All large agencies have a separate account planning function, although direct recruitment is less common than for the account executive/ manager role. Account planners try to devise the most effective strategy for galvanising the target audience. They look at economic and consumer trends, the client's own market data, market research and reports, and will tend to look at a number of different accounts at the same time to monitor strategies across the board. Account planners usually have strong numerical and analytical skills.

## Media staff

These can be in-house or part of a separate company. Diversification of the media in recent years has led to increasing specialisation among media staff in advertising. Media staff will advise clients of an appropriate format and provide a schedule of costs; in buying space they will assess the risks to be taken and negotiate a price based on knowledge of the going rate for particular kinds of product. They will also research the prominence, circulation, or viewing figures of the medium chosen. Media staff have to be good team workers with a genuine enthusiasm for advertising. They have to think quickly and have good communication skills, both written and oral. A good level of numeracy is a huge advantage.

*Creative staff*

The creative team consists of copywriters, art directors and designers. They work closely with the account management team and depend on information supplied by planners. Creative staff design advertising copy for a huge variety of outlets, from TV and cinema to mailshots and trade papers. A number of English specialists become copywriters. For this job you need to understand the consumers you are trying to motivate, to find the clearest, catchiest way of getting your message across. You will spend a lot of time working with an art director to co-ordinate words and pictures.

---

**Top Tips**

# for Getting into Advertising

◆ Spend a lot of time looking at advertisements.
◆ Talk to your friends and family about which ones work.
◆ Practise writing some copy for yourself, using a variety of formats you have seen in different media.
◆ Try it out on your friends and family.
◆ Think about which advertisements are trying to change an image rather than just sell more.
◆ Build up your own portfolio of work.
◆ Be prepared to look for openings in associated areas such as sales and marketing.
◆ Write to a local company to enquire about unpaid holiday work experience in the marketing area.
◆ Read *Campaign*, *Marketing Week* and *Marketing*.
◆ Contact the Advertising Association for specialist careers information.

---

## Case Study

**Jeremy** works as a copywriter in a West Midlands advertising agency. Most of the company's clients are manufacturers specialising in agricultural products such as fertilizers and pesticides. Jeremy's employer also has a brief to handle public relations or direct sales where appropriate.

Jeremy had always wanted to write and got a job in marketing straight after doing A-levels in English and Media Studies. It was a junior office job, but it gave him a good background in how to plan, launch, maintain and develop an advertising campaign. He was able to use his writing skills initially by contributing to his first employer's in-house magazine. After a few months he moved to a public relations agency, which increased his experience of 'being able to tell a story for the purposes of selling'. This stood him in good stead for copywriting. He also found out just how varied the profiles of people in this sector can be. One of his colleagues was an English graduate, another had no background in the humanities – just a knack for writing and a talent for getting her foot in the door at the right time (she had written a speculative application to the firm and been offered a job).

Jeremy's most recent assignment was to contribute to a campaign advertising a new method of blowfly control for sheep. This is an important area of the market as sheep-dipping goes into relative decline. Jeremy had never felt especially interested in sheep hygiene before, but he relished the challenge of writing the copy for an effective strategy. The company's creative team had decided to repackage its product by shedding its dowdy image and promoting its advantages over other solutions. Jeremy wrote headlines for the 'point of sale' displays in shops, and wrote the script for the direct mail letters which would be sent to farmers. Since this was a 'hidden product' – a chemical locked away in a shop – the creative team came up with the idea of sales assistants wearing T-shirts to advertise it. Jeremy wrote the slogan for them.

His greatest satisfaction is in seeing the end product of his work in print – on letters, posters and T-shirts – and in being able to contribute to a commercial success story. He thinks advertising in general is very much an open career where flair and determination count more than formal qualifications. He does, however, say that it is important to take every chance you can get to improve your writing skills, whether in exams or anywhere else.

## Useful addresses

**The Advertising Association**, Abford House, 15 Wilton Road, London SW1V 1NJ; 0171-828 2771

**Institute of Practitioners in Advertising**, 44 Belgrave Square, London SW1X 8QS; 0171 235 7020

*Campaign* magazine is published by Haymarket Publishing Ltd, 174 Hammersmith Road, London W6 7JP

*Marketing Week* is published by Centaur Communications Ltd, St Giles House, 50 Poland Street, London W1V 4AX; 0171 439 4222

*Marketing* magazine is published by Haymarket Business Publications Ltd, 30 Lancaster Gate, London W2 3LY

## Further reading

*The Advertising Association* publishes two useful titles: *Getting into Advertising* and *Student Briefing: Advertising*.

You should also look at the AGCAS booklets entitled *Advertising, Public Relations* and *Direct Marketing*. AGCAS also publishes a *Survey of Courses in Marketing, Advertising and Public Relations*, and has an excellent series of occupational profiles for work in this area: *Advertising and Account Executive, Advertising Account Planner, Advertising Copywriter, Media Buyer, Media Planner.*

# 4 Publishing

Like advertising, publishing covers a wide range of different occupations. There are two main categories: book publishing and magazine publishing. After the recession of the early 1990s many publishers slimmed down their structures and shed staff, which means that there is now more emphasis on freelance work. The industry is moving fast. Technological developments such as electronic and internet publishing have made computer skills more prominent than they were ten or even five years ago. On top of this, the demise of the net book agreement, which guaranteed book prices across the retail sector, will certainly affect the distribution of work in the book publishing sector. The book industry is, nonetheless, buoyant: the *Booksellers' Association Dictionary* for 1996 lists 2000 UK publishers, distributors and wholesalers, and over 8000 'imprints' (small companies owned by large publishers).

## Book publishing

Most publishing companies specialise in different markets. 50 per cent of UK sales are in 'consumer' books (ie 'trade' or 'general', including fiction and adult non-fiction, such as good pub guides, cookery books, travel guides, and so on). A further 25 per cent is taken up by educational, academic and technical books; here, a few large firms – Oxford and Cambridge University Presses, Routledge, Longman, etc – enjoy most of the market. Children's books, fiction or non-fiction, take up a further substantial share, while a growing area is multi-media publishing: some publishers, such as Dorling Kindersley, have a specialist CD-ROM depart-ment. There are other openings in book clubs and book packagers – this sounds fairly unglamorous, but such companies do produce books themselves which larger publishers pay to market. Complex illustrated books frequently come from such sources.

# The jobs

## Commissioning editor

This is close to the top of the tree, and the most popular ambi-tion for people with an interest in publishing. For non-fiction work, the commissioning editor consults with marketing and finance staff, devises a brief for a book or series, and finds people to write them. Most published books, it is worth remembering, are commissioned: the editor has therefore to make tough deci-sions about what the market wants. With fiction, the picture is different: the editor receives large numbers of unsolicited manu-scripts from literary agents or directly from authors, and has to make decisions about their quality, consistency and suitability for the market. External readers will often be asked to provide a sec-ond opinion.

To get where they are, commissioning editors need imagina-tion, good visual sense, intelligence, managerial skills, the strength of mind to say 'no' in difficult circumstances, and con-siderable diplomacy. Very few people are ready for the challenges of such a job straight away, so most will start off in one of the fol-lowing roles.

## Editorial assistant

Editorial assistants learn the basics of book publishing: typing, proof-reading, checking details, sitting in on meetings, being pre-pared to take on anything in the interests of getting noticed. They will learn to understand and evaluate processes and products before making any significant contribution themselves.

*Picture researcher*

This line of work is associated with editorial functions, and picture researchers often have English degrees. They find appropriate illustrations for books, pass information on to rights assistants (see below), mark up manuscripts for pictorial matter, and sometimes work directly from the text to develop individual ideas themselves. Picture researchers tend to work to very strict budgets, so you need to be able to compromise when you've had a bright idea.

*Desk editors*

These editors work closely with picture researchers to make the book look right. They ensure that it conforms to the publisher's house-style and supervise the process of copy-editing to make sure that everything is accurate. The desk editor may have to monitor the budget and time schedule for a book, and liaise with authors about these. Technology has made a huge difference to the desk editor's function: a great deal of copy-editing is now done by computer, while page design and styling are now done largely on disk.

*Rights managers / assistants*

Books and extracts from books are reproduced in many ways beyond the original imprint: in translation, through book clubs, multi-media, quotations in other books, and so on. Often special rights for, say, a paperback edition or distribution in the USA will be required. It is the rights manager's job to make sure that the interests of the publisher (and its authors) are respected in the process. This job requires a mind for legal niceties, a meticulous sense of detail, financial awareness, and the imagination to see new possibilities for distribution. Rights assistants may find a second language useful, since negotiating with foreign publishers is an important part of the work involved. There are a variety of routes, often from sales or advertising.

*Sales and marketing*

Nearly all book publishing is market led in some way. Publishers have to know what the demand is likely to be for a given work.

They also have to be sure that the format, price, design and promotional material are as effective as possible. This means continuous market research which editors can use to plan ahead. A number of English graduates find their way into sales and marketing as copywriters: see Chapter 3 – creative staff.

## Production

Production staff handle technical aspects of publishing: influencing and implementing decisions about design, finding the right production options for the available budget, co-ordinating production scheduling and liaising with external printers. Accuracy, numeracy and an eye for technological advances are required.

## Magazine publishing

This is a high-growth industry. Over the past ten years the number of magazines published has increased by one third. There have been qualitative developments too: the industry is diversifying to provide information electronically; there are now more foreign publishers entering the UK market; while the search for small niche markets – a long-standing feature of the industry – continues at an ever greater pace. There are about 250 magazine publishing companies, mostly in London and the South-East. The leaders in the sector are Reed Business and IPC (both subsidiaries of Reed Elsevier, which also owns Lexis-Nexis, the US business information service). Morgan Grampian, part of United Newspapers, publishes over 100 titles.

## The jobs

As with book publishing, the demarcation lines between types of work become more blurred the smaller the company. In a large firm, *editors* are more like managers, taking responsibility for the work of in-house and freelance staff, whether writers, designers or photographers; *sub-editors* will do the checking, rewriting in house style, and so on. Sub-editing is the kind of area a new graduate might enter. In a smaller company, editors are likely to be involved throughout the publishing process: liaising with senior management on overall policy; working with designers; possibly even writing themselves.

*Marketing* staff will look at target reader groups, commission and evaluate research to forecast trends, monitor the effects of editorial and sales performance, set up promotions for particular titles, and advise on advertising rates. If you are in advertising sales, you will be selling space over the telephone or by means of personal presentations. You will have to establish the client's objectives, negotiate a suitable format, and show understanding of market conditions. *Production staff* deal with advertisers' needs at the production end, check advertisement copy, make decisions about the most economical means of printing (very few magazines are printed in-house), and handle production scheduling, which sometimes includes making sure that sufficient copies get to the right distributors on time! As a production controller you need to be accurate, numerate, and have an interest in technological developments. Finally, magazines could not exist without someone taking charge of circulation: managing information about the readership and maintaining databases are key activities in the sector.

---

### Top Tips

# for Getting into Publishing

◆ Start reading the *Bookseller* magazine to get a flavour of what's going on in the industry and the kinds of jobs being advertised. Get to know the sorts of books different companies publish – their 'lists'. Catalogues are usually free. For magazine publishing, look at *Marketing Week* or *Campaign*, and buy Monday's edition of the *Guardian*.

◆ Visit the London International Book Fair and take advantage of the Society of Young Publishers' Careers Clinic.

---

◆ Work hard on your word-processing skills. A number of careers in publishing begin with secretarial-type work.

◆ Look for opportunities to work in bookshops – this can be an excellent way of getting a foot on the ladder and finding your way around sales and marketing issues.

◆ Bear in mind that a number of publishers want people with experience in particular areas: these might include working with children, teaching EFL, working in a library (indexing and cataloguing are relevant skills), speaking a foreign language, etc. Look for opportunities in these areas in the short term.

◆ Recruitment in publishing is rarely planned a long way in advance. Companies may advertise only a month or so ahead, and often only in the trade press to limit the number of applications – as someone once said, if you're not on the inside you're on the outside! There are hardly any graduate trainee schemes, so the onus is on you to familiarise yourself with the trade.

◆ The up-side of the above point is that it can pay to write speculative applications. Be prepared to send off dozens, to all levels of the industry.

◆ Work at your writing skills. Try sitting down and imitating the styles of a number of different magazines or sales catalogues. Once you've got the knack of it, collect your best work into a portfolio.

---
## Case Study
---

**Fiona** graduated with a degree in English. She spent a summer working as a part-time teacher in a language school, teaching French and Italian students on short courses. This gave her the chance to work with a range of books in an important corner of the market, and she also received some in-house teacher training. She felt that the experience prepared her for a number of future career options.

In the autumn, a Saturday job came up at the local bookshop. At interview she gave a brief presentation on different kinds of EFL books to show that she had the communication skills to help customers. They were convinced, and she got the job. Gradually she took on more work at the shop. She learned to use the computerised stock check and contributed ideas on the way book displays were organised. Her dealings with visiting sales representatives taught her a lot about how not to sell books.

The following year she saw an advertisement by a national book publisher for a trainee sales representative. The job involved travelling around bookshops in the south of England with sales catalogues and sample copies to negotiate with owners and managers over how many copies of which books they needed. On the application form she explained her experience of teaching and working in the bookshop in detail, making it clear how the skills she had developed were relevant to the new job.

She prepared for her interview by reading through the catalogues of the publisher, making a note of their best-selling titles and any new lines they were developing. A trial interview with her boyfriend boosted her confidence! On the day, she came across as efficient, knowledgeable and communicative. When she was asked to do a mock sales routine, persuading a cantankerous bookshop owner to take six copies of a book he didn't want, she got through in spite of her nerves. She was offered the job, and has since met many more cantankerous bookshop owners. She says that the variety of her job is one of its main attractions, together with the quality of the books she gets to sell. The hours are difficult – nights away from home, very early starts – but there is a great sense of freedom, at least when she is not stuck on the M25.

# Useful addresses

**Book House Training Centre**, 45 East Hill, Wandsworth, London SW18 2QZ; 0181 874 2718

**The Society of Freelance Editors and Proofreaders**, Mermaid House, 1 Mermaid Court, Borough High Street, London SE1 1HR; 0171 403 5141

**The Society of Young Publishers**, c/o J Whitaker and Sons Ltd, 12 Dyott Street, London WC1A 1DF; 0171 323 0323 (daytime) *or* 0171 740 6560 (evenings)

# Further reading

The Society of Young Publishers has a number of information sheets about careers in publishing, as well as *The Young Publisher's Handbook*. GN Clark's *Inside Book Publishing* offers a lively 'career builder's guide', as does the Kogan Page title, *Careers in Publishing and Bookselling*, by June Lines. See also the AGCAS *Survey of Printing and Publishing Courses*, and its occupational profiles for *Editor: Commissioning, Editorial Assistant, Picture Researcher*.

# 5 Journalism

Journalists work in two main areas: newspapers/magazines (print journalism) and broadcasting. Increasingly, their work is becoming more flexible and blurring the boundaries between sectors. It is still true, however, that far more journalists move from newspapers and magazines into broadcasting than the other way round. Whatever the medium, there are some basic attributes which you need to become a journalist:

◆ the ability to present information clearly in accurate English;
◆ an interest in people and an enthusiasm for current affairs;
◆ an ability to work fast and at unsocial hours;
◆ assertiveness;
◆ the knack of making sound, common-sense judgements;
◆ the courage not to back down in front of anyone except your editor!

## Print journalism

Thousands of newspapers, whether national, regional or local, appear daily, weekly or monthly; add to this figure the further thousands of consumer and business or professional magazines, and you have a huge industry. More than 60 per cent of us read a national daily, and over 90 per cent some form of local paper. Many papers are owned by large groups such as Trinity Newspapers, News Group and Express Newspapers. Not all journalists work directly for newspapers and magazines, however: 10 per cent are freelance, while a further substantial proportion work for 'wholesale' agencies such as Reuter's; in the magazine industry, up to 80 per cent of copy is written by freelance journalists. Competition to get in is tough: only about 400–600 people enter the news journalism industry each year, and most of them are graduates.

Newspaper journalists have two broad functions.

1. Gathering information – this means developing contacts, interviewing, going to public events, researching information, and producing copy to strict deadlines;
2. Preparing copy – this means, effectively, sub-editing work such as adapting copy to house-style, checking grammar, cutting to size, headline writing, planning layouts, and submitting finished material to the editor.

The same can be said of magazine journalism. Either way, it is an unpredictable way of life which by definition is at the mercy of events – definitely not for nine-to-fivers or those who want a quiet family life! Reporters spend most of their time finding out, whether on location, in archives, or on the phone. Actual writing may have to be crammed into five minutes at the end of the day. The ability to keep up contacts and sense what is relevant to the reading public are just as important as a crisp and stylistically appropriate handling of the English language.

Computer technology has already made a huge difference to the industry. Frequently journalists will file copy direct via cable link-up: this not only cuts out a number of production functions but places more onus on the writer to produce finished copy. It has become more important than ever to become computer literate and develop skills in areas of the production process other than just writing.

# The jobs

*News reporters* will do different jobs according to the kind of paper they work for. On a small local paper they might be responsible for weddings and funerals as well as burglaries and local government issues; in addition, they may well be taking the photographs and organising the layout! National reporters have a more specific brief to respond to investigative suggestions by the news desk and come up with ideas of their own.

*Specialist reporters* will work for the larger papers in a specific area, such as business, sport or the arts. They have in-depth knowledge of their area, together with the usual attributes required for reporters.

*Feature writers* produce longer, more discursive accounts of topical issues. Again, if you are a news reporter on a local paper, this might be the kind of work you have to undertake in addition to everything else. Feature writers on larger papers may specialise in, for example, health or leisure issues.

*Editorial staff* will usually be experienced journalists who make decisions about what news to cover; in a local or regional paper, they will respond to whatever agenda is being set by national publications and seek to give them a local slant. One way of starting in journalism is to become an *editorial assistant*, which involves liaising between news and other departments, and generally being prepared to mop up tasks to ensure that deadlines are met.

## Qualifications

There are a number of courses which provide training in journalism, although it must be said that none offers a guarantee of long-term employment. Most journalists have degrees in subjects like English and a good deal of practical experience. Nonetheless, the following can be recommended as good preparation for the world of journalism.

## One-year pre-entry courses

The National Council for the Training of Journalists (NCTJ) – see Useful addresses – lists available courses.

## One-year postgraduate courses

An intensive introduction run either by the NCTJ or by individual educational institutions.

## In-house training schemes

A number of newspapers, both regional and national, have their own training schemes: the *Liverpool Daily Post and Echo* and News International (which publishes *The Times*) are especially prestigious. EMAP (consumer magazines and regional dailies) also runs such a scheme.

## Case Study

**Chas** graduated in English in 1991. As an undergraduate he had worked on college magazines, arranged work experience on a local newspaper and generally kept abreast of current affairs. After finishing his degree he got on to a one-year NCTJ course at a college in Yorkshire, and at the end of the course he wrote to every local newspaper in the country to look for openings. Not all of them replied, but he did receive over 500 letters, all of which said 'no'. He wondered whether he should impart this stunning fact to The Guinness Book of Records, but decided that he couldn't cope with another letter of rejection.

Finally, just as he had completely given up hope, he got a positive response from a weekly paper in the west of England. It was a small operation: just him and another reporter, so he had to learn most tasks in the writing and production process. He gained his National Certificate after 18 months and so became senior reporter. At this point his relationship with his fellow reporter went into decline. He applied successfully for a vacancy at a nearby evening paper with a bigger circulation and bigger stories to cover: news from the magistrates' courts, environmental issues, visits of national politicians, and even a serial murderer on the loose.

After more than two years as a senior reporter he moved to the news desk to become district news editor, and then news editor. Now, he meets the editor and picture editor every morning to work out what to include for the evening's edition, where to send his reporters, and to check on copy. His next step is to become an editor or to move sideways into broadcasting. He says that you need 'an enquiring mind, to be personable, sensitive, but also persistent – a jack of all trades'. He likes being involved in making the news, but he says that the pay is, to be honest, not very good at all, and the hours are 'horrendous'.

## Broadcast journalism: radio

Radio and television are increasingly interdependent worlds, with a lot of movement between the two. Nonetheless, the structures, providers and job outlines are different – but do not expect broadcast journalism to be less pressurised than newspaper work. You will need the same stamina, willingness to work unsocial hours, and ability to think and produce quickly.

In radio, the BBC is the largest employer. It runs not only the national network (Radios 1, 2, 3, 4 and 5 Live) and the World Service, but national regional radio (eg Radio Wales) and local radio stations (Radio Hereford and Worcester, among 38 others). In addition, there are independent national stations such as Classic FM, no fewer than 140 independent local stations, and a number of satellite and cable organisations. Further expansion is likely in the near future: the release of sections of the FM spectrum creates space for up to 90 new stations, while digital audio broadcasting will improve sound quality across the FM range.

## The jobs

*Reporters* provide voice reports and taped or live interviews in whatever area they work in. They prepare bulletins to be checked by editorial staff. To be a reporter you need all the usual journalistic attributes together with a good microphone voice and a clean driving licence.

*Duty editors* do a lot of sub-editing and putting bulletins together; they collect and present information for current affairs and features programmes. Some technical competence is required. *News editors and producers* have editorial control over the station's news or current affairs output. They are responsible for making sure spending is kept within budget, for managing news staff and for linking up with other news sources at whatever level.

## Broadcast journalism: television

Television journalists also face a varied range of tasks. Off-screen, they research stories, make contacts, prepare reports, write bulletins; on-screen, they have to deliver reports, conduct interviews, and get used to working to technical and corporate requirements. Presenters and newsreaders are usually experienced journalists and often write their own scripts. Anybody who works in front of the cameras needs to be able to think quickly and remain calm at all costs.

News editors and their assistants decide which stories to cover in what proportions, and allocate reporters and camera crews accordingly. They check the quality of copy submitted, work to very tight deadlines and need to be able to adapt to rapidly changing circumstances. The overall managerial responsibility is taken by the programme editor, who monitors budgets, personnel and the style of the product.

## Training

Getting into print journalism first is your best bet. For editorial and production aspects of broadcasting there are trainee schemes, but these are highly competitive (up to 600 applicants for each place in one instance) and offer no guarantee of work afterwards. To stand any chance of being considered for one of these courses you will need a degree and some experience in media, excellent interpersonal skills, an innovative mind, a very good grasp of current affairs, and a good deal of stamina. If this doesn't put you off, try:

◆ The BBC Production Trainee Scheme;
◆ The BBC Network Radio Production Trainee Scheme;
◆ BBC World Service Production Trainee Scheme;
◆ Granada Trainee Programme Maker Scheme.

See also some of the titles in the Further reading section to find out more.

---

### Top Tips

## for Getting into Journalism

◆ Work on a student magazine. If there isn't one at your school, college or university, start one!
◆ Many local newspapers use 'stringers' or local correspondents to report on minor events such as school news. Write to your local paper and ask about this kind of work. Be persistent.
◆ Ask about work placements in local papers. Offer to do chores such as sorting out the cuttings file. Ask about shadowing a member of staff.
◆ Learn word-processing and shorthand skills – aim to reach a hundred words a minute for shorthand.
◆ Write speculative applications – most jobs in journalism are not advertised. If you think you'll be put off by receiving too many rejection letters, read the case study for print journalism on page 28.

---

### Case Study

**Janey** graduated ten years ago. She'd been active in her college drama society and was a generally sociable, popular person. She had big ideas for a career: broadcasting, the city, maybe politics. She applied for the BBC's production trainee programme, certain of success. When a letter from 'Auntie' fell on to the doormat one morning she rushed to open it, ready to break open the champagne, only to read the sort of well-meaning but brief letter of rejection which, she later realised, several hundred other hopefuls had also received. What else was there to do?

She went for an aptitude test at the careers centre, and had an interview with an adviser. These established that some form of career in journalism was what she really wanted, so it was now a question of finding out where to start. She returned home to live with her parents (because it was cheaper), and wrote to all the local papers asking about work experience or job shadowing, with one positive response. She got a month's experience during the summer filing press clippings and starting to load material on to a computer. She aimed to make herself indispensable, but at the end of the month she had not succeeded, so she made follow-up telephone calls to all the other newspapers.

Now, though, she had some practical experience, and she got an office job with a paper in the next town. The work was similar to what she had done before, but eventually, after pestering the editor, she was sent out to cover minor local news stories from petty theft to cats in distress. After six months she was well placed to cover the maternity leave of a senior colleague, and began to write property features, liaising with local estate agents and writing up descriptions of any unusual or desirable houses for sale in the area.

Janey had been doing this job for nearly a year when she saw an advertisement for a reporter on a financial magazine in London. The work was specialised, requiring knowledge of current affairs and a certain amount of economic know-how. She mugged up desperately, relying a lot on her knowledge of the property market and the fluctuating economic conditions which affected it. When she was invited for a interview, she was so afraid of being caught out that she nearly didn't go. The interview was, she says, 'like skating on thin ice', but she got the job. Afterwards she found out that she had been successful because they had admired her nerve!

Nerve was certainly required when she was working for the magazine. One of her first assignments was to interview the Danish finance minister about his country's economic policy with regard to the European Union. More desperate mugging! It was like 'living on a tightrope', but also, she observes, strangely like preparing for a college assignment. She couldn't quite foresee a time when she would be entirely confident of not being thought a complete fool, so she went back to her original ambition of getting into broadcasting. She applied again for the BBC production trainee scheme, and this time, with her considerable experience of print journalism, got a place. She thinks she is still square-eyed from watching all that television in preparation for the interview.

Her first full job was on the production team of a financial programme, but by now she was sure that she wanted to have a more general current affairs brief. She transferred to a documentary team, and now does a job share with her husband, also a producer – six weeks on, six weeks off. The six weeks on are, she says, 'incredibly hectic', and she sometimes works 15 hours a day to make sure that production schedules are met.

She has to supervise filming, oversee the production of a script, co-ordinate the work of different technical departments, and generate new ideas for future programmes, with costings and organisational details attached.

She summarises the value of her degree to her present work in these terms: 'developing my personal organisation, forcing me to write to very tight deadlines, and giving me a sense of personal goals'.

# Useful addresses

**Newspaper Society Training Department**, Bloomsbury House, Bloomsbury Square, 74–77 Great Russell Street, London WC1B 3DA; 0171 636 7014

**The National Council for the Training of Journalists (NCTJ)**, Latton Bush Centre, Southern Way, Harlow, Essex CM18 7BL; 01279 430009

**Scottish Newspapers Publishers' Association**, 48 Palmerston Place, Edinburgh EH12 5DE; 0131 220 4353

**Periodicals Training Council (PTC)**, Queen's House, 55/56 Lincoln's Inn Fields, London WC2A 3LJ; 0171 404 4168

**National Council for Training of Broadcast Journalists (NCTBJ)**, c/o Mr Gordon Parker, Secretary, 188 Lichfield Court, Sheen Road, Richmond, Surrey TW9 1BB; 0181 940 0694

**BBC Recruitment Services**, 201 Wood Lane, London W12 7TS; 0171 580 4468

**Independent Television News**, 200 Gray's Inn Road, London WC1X 8XZ; 0171 843 8000

**Skillset**, 124 Horseferry Road, London SW1P 2TX; 0171 306 8585

**The National Union of Journalists (NUJ)**, 314 Gray's Inn Road, London WC1X 8DP; 0171 278 7916

# Further reading

Angell, Robert *How to Get into Films and TV* (How To Books, 1994)
*Benn's Media Directory* (Benn Bros, 1996)
*Journalism and Writing* (AGCAS Graduate Careers Information)
*Magazine Journalism* (Periodicals Training Council, 1996)
*Willing's Press Guide* (Reed Information Services, 1996)
Niblock, Sarah *Inside Journalism* (Blueprint, 1994)
Selby, Michael *Careers in TV and Radio* (Kogan Page, 1994)
*The Official ITV Careers Handbook* (Hodder & Stoughton, 1992)

In addition, the Newspaper Society publishes a booklet called *Training to be a Journalist*, the PTC issues *Careers in Magazines*, while AGCAS publishes a *Survey of Postgraduate Courses in Journalism*. The NUJ has a useful guide called *Careers in Journalism*. For insights into the daily lives of journalists, see the following AGCAS occupational profiles: *Journalist, Broadcasting*; *Journalist, Magazine*; *Journalist, Newspaper*; *Sub-editor, Press*.

Finally, look out for another Kogan Page title, *Careers in Journalism* by Simon Kent.

# Teaching in schools and colleges

This chapter covers primary and secondary school teaching, with a few words on university and college teaching. See Chapter 7 for Teaching English as a Foreign Language. Note that all the details about recruitment, numbers and training procedures given here apply only to England and Wales. See the list of useful addresses at the end of this section for information relating to Scotland and Northern Ireland.

Between 25,000 and 30,000 newly qualified primary and secondary teachers are needed every year to maintain the national total of 440,000 qualified professionals. Add to this the fact that the number of teaching posts has risen substantially over the past four years, and that there will still be a shortage of trained teachers during the next four years, and you have a growing area to consider. For PGCE secondary English alone, there is to be a 10 per cent increase in the number of places offered next year. As with everything else, however, be warned: there is stiff competition to get on to postgraduate and first degree teacher training courses.

A number of well-publicised changes have taken place in the education system in England and Wales:

◆ testing at ages seven, 11 and 14 (there are proposals for testing five-year-olds as well!);
◆ performance league tables to indicate which schools have the 'best' overall results;
◆ the possibility of increasing self-management among schools.

You need to acquaint yourself with the details and implications of these changes if you are persuade an interview panel that you would make a responsible teacher. See Further reading, at the end of this section.

Apart from the age of the children, the chief difference between primary and secondary teaching is that at primary level you have to teach all the National Curriculum subjects, including English, maths, science and technology, and a range of creative and social skills; in addition, there are foundation subjects such as history, geography, IT, music, art and physical education. In the secondary classroom, you generally specialise in the subject you studied at degree level. All teachers should have the ability to do something else besides this. You need also to exercise care, patience, impeccable organisation and preparation, curiosity and enthusiasm with a diverse group of children, some of whom may not be all that pleasant on first acquaintance. Many people who consider teaching say that they like children, on the basis of having played with one or two nieces or nephews. The important thing to remember is that they behave differently in a large group! There are ways of finding out if involvement in young people's activities is for you: summer activity holidays, play schemes and play groups, youth organisations, even American summer camps. Far more than the necessary reading, such as the National Curriculum documents or *The Times Educational Supplement* (both should be available from your local library), direct experience of working with children will tell you whether teaching is the career you are after. Last of all, remember that teaching, like many other worthwhile careers, is not a nine-to-five job: preparation, marking, parents' evenings and extracurricular activities have a way of eating into spare time. The demands on time have certainly increased with the changes in education mentioned above.

The rewards, however, are substantial, at least in non-material ways.

# Primary level teaching

Primary teachers help children with:

◆ reading and writing;
◆ understanding mathematical concepts;
◆ learning about science and technology;
◆ learning about history and culture in different settings;
◆ developing curiosity and the capacity for rational thinking;
◆ acquiring social skills and an awareness of other ways of life;
◆ developing creativity through art, drama and music.

Teachers also contribute to the personal, moral and health education of their classes. To teach successfully at this level you must be:

◆ completely on top of the material covered;
◆ a good communicator;
◆ creative and energetic;
◆ flexible enough to respond to changes in the curriculum and to the make up of different year groups;
◆ always aware of substantial variations in ability among the children.

# Training

The main route into primary teaching is via a BEd or BA (QTS) degree (QTS stands for 'Qualified Teacher Status'). This will last three or four years, depending on the institution. The A-level grades you need will vary likewise. Bear in mind that if you start primary training after 1 September 1998 you will need a science GCSE as well as the standard requirements of maths and English language GCSE. You can choose to specialise in one of three different age ranges: 3–5, 5–7 or 7–11. Thirty-two weeks of a four-year BEd would be spent in schools (this amounts to a whole academic year of practical training). The overwhelming majority of teacher training establishments will see to it that you have experience of a wide range of schools, from the 'high achieving' to the 'difficult' – you should not expect to have it easy just because you are still learning how to do the job!

For a primary PGCE, you will need a good degree as well as the GCSE qualifications outlined above. Any subject is technically valid, but increasingly the trend is to favour people with a degree in a National Curriculum subject: as an English graduate, you will be well placed. During your one-year course you could expect to spend 18 weeks in schools.

## Case Study

**Trudi** studied English at a northern university and graduated in 1991. Her decision to go into teaching was a gradual one. She first started thinking about it when she met a group of BEd students in her first year, but the key moment was the discovery of just how few job opportunities there were in the summer of 1991! She applied for a place on the PGCE upper primary course at a neighbouring university and was accepted.

Within five weeks of starting the course, she was in the classroom for a month on her first placement. This was a real eye-opener. She had not realised how much planning and evaluation was involved, and this when the National Curriculum was still in its infancy. One afternoon per week was spent on different core National Curriculum subjects such as maths and science, and there were two sessions on dance. It was very hard work, not eased by the fact that Trudi had to support herself with bar work at the same time. The course was very intensive and worthwhile, but Trudi points out that 'it takes a good three years to actually understand how children learn'.

Her first job was in an inner-city primary school. She was appalled by the problems which many of her eight-year-olds brought with them from home. Nonetheless, her colleagues were very supportive and the school maintained a warm atmosphere: for many of the children, school was a cheerful and orderly alternative to home. Her initial contract was for one year, but she was offered an extension towards the end of the year. She decided, however, to move south, where many of her friends were living. 'Teaching gives you a certain mobility', she says.

Her new catchment area formed a complete contrast to her previous urban environment – it was 'leafy, rural, and middle class', and her new school was the first to win one of the government's Charter Marks. Her job was to teach infants, which was very challenging because she had had no training in organising and delivering 'an integrated day'. She also did some teaching in the upper years. After her first year she offered to act as art co-ordinator and to be responsible for wall displays, but was

advised by the Headteacher to take on a National Curriculum core subject as well to make herself more marketable. Heeding this advice, she
spent the next 18 months shadowing the maths co-ordinator and took on
the role after his departure to another job. She is currently supporting this
by studying part time for an MEd, financed by her local authority. Sharing
ideas and developing material with fellow professionals has been very
stimulating for her.

Trudi summarises the rewards in these terms: 'you get out of it just
what you put in'; 'you're your own boss once the door's shut'; 'if the Red
Arrows are flying over you can seize the opportunity to make it a source
for your lesson'; 'working in a primary school is being part of a little community'. Once one of her friends, a solicitor, was rash enough to say that
being a primary school teacher wasn't a real job. Trudi invited her to
spend a day in the classroom, and by 3.30 her friend was exhausted and
had to concede that Trudi was just as much a professional as she was.
Trudi then told her about all the work she had to do that evening.

---

# Secondary level teaching

There are over 4000 state-funded secondary schools in the UK.
People who teach in them have many of the same skills, and
experience many of the same problems, as those in the primary
sector. The difference is that there is a greater emphasis on pass-
ing knowledge on to your classes: to do that with enthusiasm,
variety and flexibility offers a greater intellectual challenge. In
recent years encouragement has also been given to the need to
integrate all children within mainstream linguistic culture. The
National Curriculum states that:

> 'English should develop pupils' abilities to communicate effec-
> tively in speech and writing and to listen with understanding. It
> should also enable them to be enthusiastic, responsive and knowl-
> edgeable readers. In order to participate confidently in public, cul-
> tural and working life, pupils need to be able to speak, write and
> read standard English fluently and accurately.'

It follows that as a prospective teacher you should have some
knowledge of the background to and implications of this important and controversial statement. See, for example, the discussions
of 'Standard English' in Ronald Wardhaugh's *An Introduction to*

*Sociolinguistics* (Blackwell, 1986), and M Stubbs's *Language, Schools and Classrooms* (Methuen, 1985). Wherever you stand on this question, the National Curriculum remains!

It is worth stressing the variety of secondary English teaching. As well as the opportunity to immerse yourself in different kinds of reading matter and dramatic material, there are many writing skills to teach and encourage.

## Life after teaching?

We have tried to stress over and over again the need to be flexible in your career plans. Chapter 4 suggests that one route into publishing is via teaching. At first sight it may seem a little cynical to imply that you should consider teacher training as the first step to some other career, teaching being by definition to many of us a vocation. A knowledge of practical education is, nonetheless, useful in many areas of the economy beyond the classroom. Many teachers take their skills into other careers, often to the general benefit of the education system. Apart from movement within or up the profession – such as educational management, counselling or inspection – a significant number of trained, experienced teachers may find themselves working as education officers for cultural organisations or for local government, as journalists, or in some other area of the media. Teachers are highly valued for their presentational and organisational skills, and do well outside their first profession as long as they are prepared to be flexible.

---
### Case Study
---

For most of his school career **Roger** really disliked his teachers. He could not understand why they wanted to do a job like that, but supposed it was something to do with needing to order people around, and largely failing. He did love reading, however. When it came to deciding what to do after A-levels, he was torn between studying English at university and doing something more vocational, like law or accounting (his maths had always been good). What finally decided him in favour of English was that his parents wanted him to do accounting.

He did well at university and obtained a good degree. His tutors always said that he was very well organised and disciplined, but that he lacked originality in his approach. This depressed him and made him wonder whether any sort of career connected with literature was really for him. He couldn't be sure. Added to that, he had enjoyed a rather comfortable upbringing and didn't like the idea of being poorly paid for years. So, to the bewilderment of his parents, he enrolled on a postgraduate accountancy course. He couldn't get a grant to do this, so he worked during the summer and part time throughout the postgraduate year and managed to support himself, if only just. Soon after he finished, he got a junior job in a local accountant's. They liked the way he dealt with clients; his articulate and personable manner seemed to set him apart from some people who had been dreaming of accountancy since the cradle. Or was he flattering himself?

Two years passed, and Roger began to sense that nothing had really changed since he'd begun his job. There were more exams to complete, but the effort didn't seem worthwhile. He could answer the question of what he was doing this for (money), but not who he was doing it for. He realised that what he really wanted was to make some difference to the world – to help people think about something other than their bank accounts. A telephone call to his local College of Higher Education revealed that there was a one-year PGCE course in English, and he took the plunge. His first degree qualified him technically, and his experience of work made him an even more attractive prospect for the profession. Work had, he found during his teaching practice, also made him more confident with other people; some of his fellow trainees suffered in the rougher placements, but he always came through. He saw the potential of English teaching to open children's minds to perspectives beyond their everyday lives and circumstances. This was why he had always loved reading: to help others share the same excitement was the most worthwhile feeling of all.

Six months into his first job, on a salary just over half of what he had been earning before his change of direction, he bumped into his old boss in the supermarket. The accountancy business was struggling a little; business rates had gone up, quite a few clients had gone bust, and the future looked bleak. Roger's tale wasn't all rosy either. His school was to be inspected by OFSTED in two months, and the paperwork and meetings constantly encroached on his spare time. He was also involved in the school play, which meant staying after hours three nights a week. There was barely enough time for marking and preparation. Nonetheless, he could say that he was still enjoying it, and that he could see the point of what he was doing. He had really started to wonder about all those old teachers of his he had so disliked.

# Useful addresses

For general information on teaching:

**Department for Education and Employment (DfEE)**, Sanctuary Buildings, Great Smith Street, London SW1P 3BT; 0171 925 5000

The DfEE also has a publications centre at PO Box 8927, London E3 3NZ; 0171 5100150

**Teacher Training Agency (TTA)**, TTA Communications Centre, PO Box 3210, Chelmsford, Essex CM1 3WA. (There is an information line at this address on 01245 454454.)

The ECCTIS 2000 computer database lists all teacher training courses in the UK. You will also find a complete list of such courses England and Wales in:

*The Handbook of Initial Teacher Training in England and Wales*, published by: **National Association of Teachers in Further and Higher Education (NATFHE)**, 27 Britannia Street, London WC1X 9JP; 0171 837 3636

To apply for a BEd or BA QTS course in England or Wales contact:

**The University and College Admissions Service (UCAS)**, Fulton House, Jessop Avenue, Cheltenham, Gloucestershire GL50 3SH; 01242 222444

To apply for a PGCE course in England or Wales you must contact:

**The Graduate Teacher Training Agency (GTTR)**, Fulton House, Jessop Avenue, Cheltenham, Gloucestershire GL50 3SH; 01242 225868

If you wish to teach in Scotland, apply to:

**Teacher Education Admissions Clearing House**, PO Box 165, Edinburgh EH8 8AT; 0131 5386169/70

For Northern Ireland, contact:

**Department for Education in Northern Ireland**, Balloo Road, Bangor, County Down BT19 7PR, Northern Ireland; 01247 279537

Other organisations which offer free information about careers in teaching include trade unions.

**The National Association of Schoolmasters and Union of Women Teachers (NASUWT)**, Hillscourt Education Centre, Rose Hill, Rednal, Birmingham B45 8RS; 0121 453 6150

**The National Association of Teachers in Further and Higher Education (NATFHE)**, 27 Britannia Street, London WC1X 9PJ; 0171 837 3636

Information about grants and loans can be gained from your local authority education department and from the following:

**Students' Awards Agency for Scotland**, Gyleview House, 3 Redheughs Rigg, Edinburgh EH12 9HH; 0131 244 5823

**Student Loans Company Ltd**, 100 Bothwell Street, Glasgow G2 7JI; Freephone 0800 405010 or 0141 248 8000

Opportunities to work in the private sector can be investigated through:

**The Independent Schools Information Service (ISIS)**, 56 Buckingham Gate, London SW1E 6AG; 0171-630 8793

## Further reading

AGCAS publishes a number of useful books in this area. See *Survey of Selection Criteria and Procedures for Secondary PGCE Courses in Non-National Curriculum Courses; Survey of Selection Criteria and Procedures for Primary PGCE Courses; So You Want to Teach?; Teaching in Schools and Colleges in the UK.*

See also another Kogan Page title, *Careers in Teaching* by Felicity Taylor.

# 7 Teaching English as a foreign language

Here's a good party question: what is Britain's biggest export? Not Jaguar cars, financial services, or telecommunications systems. The answer, believe it or not, is English language teaching. This is not so surprising when you consider that 70 per cent of the world's mail is in English, that English is the language of international business, that it is the second language of an increasing number of countries, and, furthermore, that with advances in information and communications technology, the English language is still growing! There is still a huge global demand for EFL teachers, one sign of which is that it remains possible to establish a healthy career in this area with comparatively little preparation or experience. Many careers prove to be stepping-stones to other careers. This is particularly true of EFL teaching, although an increasing number of people stay in it throughout their working lives, turning the proverbial 'extended holiday' into a serious and rewarding career. Two distinct kinds of teaching are involved. 'TEFL' means teaching the language to people in or from other countries for their personal, business or professional needs. 'TESL' (Teaching English as a Second Language), sometimes called 'TESOL' (Teaching English to Speakers of Other Languages), involves helping ethnic minorities and others to take a full part in the mainstream culture of their adopted homeland; it may also extend to countries such as Nigeria or Singapore where English enjoys a semi-official status.

Within those two broad areas the range of employment options is considerable, as the following examples show.

1. Private language schools employ large numbers of young teachers, many of them relatively inexperienced, during the summer high season, when London, Oxford, Cambridge and the south coast resorts are particularly vibrant. Recruitment at other times of the year is rather less generous.
2. There are public sector opportunities too, although here the likelihood is that more qualifications and experience will be needed. Local education authorities may arrange special courses according to needs in the area, while schools, colleges and universities very often have to make provision for non-native speaking pupils and students. In higher education there is a seasonal late summer boom as in the private sector; once again, permanent employment is more competitive.
3. The overseas market is, of course, the largest and most diverse: state and private schools; language schools; industry; colleges and universities and so on. There are a number of state-sponsored schemes, such as the Japanese Education Ministry's JET programme for graduates. Most of the work offered overseas will be for limited periods, so the EFL teacher's life is necessarily itinerant (precisely what draws many people to it). Only the British Council tends to offer longer-term security; competition for jobs with them is accordingly stiff. For posts available overseas, look at *The Times Educational Supplement,* Tuesday's *Guardian, EFL Gazette,* and *Overseas Jobs Express.*

## The skills you need

EFL teachers need to be:

◆ energetic, imaginative, and prepared to show off a bit;
◆ interested in other people and cultures;
◆ good at dealing with people in groups;
◆ able to get other people talking – language teachers are primarily facilitators rather than instructors; learners learn through practice, not by being talked at;

◆ able to think of simple ways to demonstrate meanings – if you are good at charades, this may well be the career for you;

◆ possessed of a clear speaking voice;

◆ willing to spend hours preparing the right level of material for each group you teach – there's nothing more dispiriting for learners than doing exercises which are either too easy or too difficult;

◆ interested in other languages, although this is not as important for EFL teachers as being willing to work at their knowledge of their own language.

In many ways this last is the biggest challenge. Try this simple test for starters. Compare the sentences, 'He went for a short walk' and 'He slept long and deep'. Would you say that 'short' and 'long' are both adjectives, both adverbs, or is one an adjective and the other an adverb? Could you explain why? Don't give up if you're completely bamboozled! Try looking through the *Collins Cobuild English Grammar* and raise your awareness of rules and structures.

As with any area of teaching, there are administrative openings once a sufficient apprenticeship has been served: course managers, directors of studies, and so on. Such jobs entail taking overall responsibility for the planning and delivery of teaching.

## How to get in

It is possible to teach English abroad without specialist training. There are organisations which recruit in this way. However, it is advisable to undergo some formal preparation first. Some language schools run their own training courses for people preparing to teach there. Details of these may be found in the *ELT Directory*, a copy of which should be in your careers or public library. In addition, there is a 'home tuition' scheme based in larger cities which allows you to work as a volunteer ESL teacher. This is an excellent way of gaining experience. However, the two most respected and marketable courses for beginners are the RSA/UCLES Certificate

(Royal Society of Arts/University of Cambridge Local Examinations Certificate), sometimes referred to as the RSA Cert, and the Trinity College Certificate. They are four to five week courses offering an intensive introduction to the theory and practice of language teaching, and are very often held at private language schools. There is also an RSA Certificate in Teaching English as a Second Language to Adults. The cost can be high for such a short course. UCLES and Trinity courses may demand up to £1000, but remember that this partly reflects the expectation that you may be going straight into employment afterwards. Some courses may attract funding from the Training and Enterprise Council.

It must be stressed that these are initial qualifications only – something to take the depth out of the deep end, so to speak. If you want to pursue a serious career in TEFL you should consider, after appropriate teaching experience, a Diploma from RSA/UCLES or Trinity College; an MA in Applied Linguistics (only possible after a first degree or substantial experience of teaching); or a PGCE course with a TEFL/TESOL option (send off for details to the Graduate Teacher Training Agency, whose address is on p 42). Under the listings of the University and College Admissions Service (addresses on p 42), you may also find some first-degree courses with modules or options in TEFL.

---
## Case Study
---

**Sara** left school with A-levels in French and English. A bright, sociable person, she was a good communicator and popular with everyone. Even though most of her friends were off to college or university, she didn't want to continue studying straight away. She took occasional jobs for a few months, working behind a bar, helping out in a clothes shop, and generally looking around for ideas.

The following summer she saw an advertisement in her local paper from a language school which wanted people to help out with their social programme. This meant taking groups of Spanish and Italian students around places of interest, near and far, making sure they were safe and had a good time. She applied, impressed the school with her confident and friendly manner, and got the job. She had to book coaches, arrange group discounts for visits to castles, cinemas, sporting events and restaurants, and accompany the students. It was interesting to talk to them about their own cultures and their impressions of Britain, and she was delighted to discover that she had no difficulty in communicating with them. After a fortnight, on one of her free days, the course manager phoned her to ask if she could step in for a teacher who had suddenly fallen ill. 'Just take a newspaper article and talk about it with them,' he said. Sara was a little unsure, but agreed anyway. It was a revelatory two hours. She found it very difficult to explain some of the rules the students asked her about (they seemed to know more about the English language than she did), but it was great fun simply getting them all talking and trying out their practical English skills. By the end of the session, she felt close to the students and, somehow, closer to herself.

Once the summer was over, she applied to Trinity College London to do their intensive Certificate course. Intensive certainly proved to be the word. Thirty hours a week for five weeks she crammed theoretical ideas, did dreadfully embarrassing group exercises, and was let loose on classes of real, live students. It seemed like torture, a return to school exams; but it was also exhilarating and gave her a sense of how much she could learn about this kind of career. She seemed to be especially good at getting shy students talking, which was very satisfying. On top of this, she felt a great sense of group identity with her peers.

A few months passed after her course had finished. It seemed to be a quiet time for jobs. She kept looking in the *EFL Gazette*, but there was nothing for someone of her experience which she liked the look of. Eventually, an advertisement appeared for a job in a private language school in Greece. They were offering a reasonable salary and tied accommodation. The hours were long but she was prepared for hard work. She applied, using her old Trinity College tutor as a referee, and was asked to an interview at a language school in London. She had been warned in advance that she would have to give a demonstration class as part of the interview, so she put something together based on work covered during her Certificate course. She got the job.

It wasn't what she had expected. Many of the students were training to be cooks or waiters, and although they were all very polite and friendly they were not seriously interested in learning English. Teaching materials were restricted, so Sara ended up writing a lot herself. She was grateful that her Certificate course had given her some introduction to how to do that. The school day began at 7.30 am and ended at 4 pm. She was scheduled to do an average of 21 lessons per week, but there was also much preparation. Eighteen months later, she moved on.

After six years and three different Mediterranean countries, Sara decided it was time to get better qualified. She applied for a sandwich MA in Applied Linguistics at a British university. Her practical experience was accepted in lieu of a first degree. The two-year sandwich course allowed her to study by correspondence for the first part of the year and return to Britain for the taught components after Easter. Her employers, a language school in Italy, supported her morally but not financially. It was sometimes very frustrating to go over complex theories of grammar and lexis when she believed she already knew what they meant in practice. The course ended up being worth while, however, and qualified her to apply for a long-term job teaching for the British Council in an Eastern European country which had recently introduced English as its official second language in place of Russian. This was a completely new challenge which involved teaching businessmen and academics as well as private individuals. She has particular responsibility for a course in English for Business Purposes, which runs alongside initiatives to develop free-market economics in this former Soviet bloc nation. This gives her a taste of what it might be like to become a Director of Studies when the right opening comes up; on the other hand, having learned the basics of two or more European languages may be useful to her for other purposes.

---

# Useful addresses

**British Council English Language Information Centre**, Medlock Street, Manchester M15 4AA; 0161 957 7000

**National Association for the Teaching of English and other Community Languages to Adults**, South Birmingham College, 524 Stratford Road, Birmingham B11 4AJ; 0121 694 5070

**Royal Society of Arts (RSA) Examinations Board**, Westwood Way, Coventry CV4 8HS; 01203 470033

**Trinity College London**, 16 Park Crescent, London W1N 4AP; 0171 323 2328

**University of Cambridge Local Examinations (UCLES)**, Hills Road, Cambridge CB1 2EU; 01223 553789

# Further reading

*The ELT Guide* (EFL Ltd, 1996)

Harmer, Jeremy *The Practice of English Language Teaching* (Longman, 1983)

Jones, Roger *How to Teach Abroad* (How to Books, 1994)

Lee McKay, Sandra *Teaching English Overseas* (OUP, 1992)

The AGCAS booklet *Teaching English as a Foreign Language and Teaching English Abroad* is also useful. For more information on the daily life of the EFL teacher, see the AGCAS occupational profile, *Teacher, English as a Foreign Language.*

The British Council publishes a number of helpful pamphlets: *Academic Courses in TEFL – RSA Certificate; Academic Courses in TEFL – RSA Diploma; Employment in TEFL; How to Become a Teacher of English as a Foreign Language.*

# 8 Arts administration

This is one of the most exciting and challenging areas for anyone with an arts background. You will be the envy of your friends and derive constant satisfaction from contributing to the nation's cultural life, as well as to any number of worthy local initiatives. Rubbing shoulders with actors, directors, musicians and painters, you can savour the glamour of that unforgettable first-night atmosphere.

You will also find that arts administration is one of the most competitive, insecure and badly paid sectors mentioned in this book. Infinite flexibility, negotiating skills, sensitivity to other people's views, a willingness to work very long hours (often over the weekend), and a watertight instinct for organisation are essential. Arts administrators may be front-of-house managers, fundraisers, marketeers, programmers, educational co-ordinators, tour operators, or all six rolled into one. They may be responsible for personnel and premises, for contractual matters, for office resources, for booking tours, for liaising with funding bodies, and for budgeting and financial control. The old rule applies: the smaller the operation, the more diverse the job.

All arts bodies – nationally and locally – are having to think increasingly commercially. At the same time, the major source of funding for a large number of arts organisations remains the Arts Councils of England, Scotland, Wales and Northern Ireland. Each of these is funded by the Department of National Heritage. Although Arts Council funding has been severely restricted for more than ten years, the National Lottery has created extra revenue, running into hundreds of millions of pounds, resulting in a growth in project development work and an increased number of staff at the Arts Councils engaged in assessing it. The terms of Lottery funding are subject to current review, with the trend inclining towards more locally based projects, away from the metropolitan and 'elite' centres.

There is another side to the coin. Arts administrators do not only work for arts organisations; many of them are employed by central or local government. Local policy is developed and implemented by the thirteen Regional Arts Boards (RABs) of England and Wales, who work with a variety of public and private bodies including the British Film Institute, local authorities, the Crafts Council and commercial sponsors. Each RAB has a director and assistant plus officers in charge of individual areas such as music, crafts and film, although there does seem to be a move away from such specialisation. In addition, many local authorities employ arts administrators or community arts officers to help in fundraising, supporting local groups, assisting in the drafting of bids, and other such tasks. In the government side of arts administration, decisions about funding and planning are often crucially linked to broader considerations of social policy: there is no 'pure' artistic quest for truth or glory!

Overall, whichever side of the industry you are on, it is a precarious living which can let you down no matter how creative and enterprising you are (and you will have to be high up on the scale on both counts to get started). Short-term contracts are becoming more common, and it is an equivocal benefit that the only increase in available jobs is for people to help raise money for the arts. It seems increasingly likely, too, that RABs (like many other organisations) will use specialist outside agencies in the future.

## The jobs

*Marketing*
Much the same as anywhere – see Chapter 10.

*Financial Management*

To quote a well-known saying, financial management in the arts is not so much about managing on a shoe-string as trying to tie bits of shoe-string together. It is as important to plan cash flow as it is to make creative proposals: you need good numeracy, planning skills and imagination. There is currently a growth in 'project' or 'development' management, which involves working for a fixed term – to renovate a venue, for example.

*Programming*

This means deciding what events to put on, perhaps drawing up contracts for bookings, and sometimes (this is the good bit) attending concerts and performances to decide what to book.

*House management*

The house manager takes reponsibility for the building – health and safety matters, for repairs and maintenance, whatever catering facilities there may be, and the running of the box office.

*Community arts officer*

This involves working for local government, often in 'deprived' areas or enabling people to get involved with non-traditional art forms such as juggling, making video films, or street theatre. It often entails liaison with schools, youth leaders and social workers.

Other areas in arts administration include:

◆ *promoters* (companies who put up money for events or productions and make decisions about where they should happen and who should be in them);
◆ *agents* (small companies who find work for performers);
◆ *fixers* (small companies who specialise in finding musicians for concerts or sessions).

---

### Top Tips

## for Getting into Arts Administration

What you need above all is experience of some kind. The following tips show how you can obtain this.

◆ Find out about community arts projects in your area and ask if you can assist or shadow the administrator(s) involved on a voluntary basis. You can start finding out about where things are happening by writing to the Arts Council (see Useful addresses, below):

◆ Find out about any local festivals – arts or more general ones – and get yourself on to the committee by volunteering ideas and assistance.

◆ Get involved in student performances/productions and contribute to the management side – selling tickets, planning advertising, arranging a small tour, selling the show to local schools.

◆ Gain some work experience – it does not have to be directly related – which will enable you to demonstrate practical financial skills when the right opportunity turns up (the same goes for any experience which involves you in raising money).

---

When you have some experience to offer in this overcrowded marketplace, look out for jobs in *Arts Management Weekly*, the *Guardian, Stage and TV Today*, or simply in your local or regional paper. Remember that many jobs in arts administration start off as voluntary, part-time or fixed-term assignments.

---

### Case Study

**Clare** read English at college. She knew that she wanted to work in the arts, although not in a creative capacity. On graduating, she signed up for a secretarial course since, she says, 'Computing skills are pretty well essential for anyone wanting to work in arts administration'. At the same time she began to forge links with local arts organisations by doing voluntary work such as taking theatre posters around local shops and pushing leaflets through letter-boxes. Then she got her first job! She became a temp, but not in an arts organisation. She just wanted to be able to prove that she wasn't a novice when it came to office work. After a year she gained her first arts post, working for the Eastern Arts Board (EAB), the regional development agency for the East of England. She was appointed literature assistant, working alongside the literature officer. She had to answer phone calls and letters about getting published or obtaining funding. She managed a scheme whereby aspiring writers could have their manuscripts reviewed by professionals, which meant running a budget, corresponding with those involved and arranging convenient schedules. She arranged meetings for her boss, and went with her to several important conferences and planning sessions. As she progressed she took part in appraisals of clients, managed bigger budgets, and was allowed to set up new schemes. She particularly enjoyed 'working for something worthwhile' and being able to help people develop skills and interests. The only problem was that she never felt secure because of the precarious state of public funding; she was also on the sharp end a few times when hopeful clients didn't get the money they had hoped for!

After four and a half years, she decided that she needed broader experience of arts administration and to work with forms other than literature. Unusually in this area, she negotiated voluntary redundancy which would enable her to undertake more voluntary work and so diversify her portfolio. This was a brave step, and some of her colleagues were doubtful. To her delight, a job was advertised at the Cambridge Arts Theatre. She was interviewed, thought she did well, but didn't get it. The rejection letter was, nonetheless, encouraging, so she pestered the theatre management to take her on as a volunteer. She started to work four days a week, unpaid, in the marketing department. The remaining day she spent in paid work with the local authority as a freelance literature promotion officer. This was similar to her EAB job: she arranged a mini-festival of literature, started a reading group in the local prison, and programmed a series of poetry readings in local pubs. She also worked as a secretary in the Development Office of a Cambridge College, which was a great introduction to fund-raising and an inimitable database called 'Raiser's Edge'.

Now she is freelancing on a range of arts marketing projects, relying on contacts and contacts' contacts. Her work includes answering questions about funding and helping to compile reports on market research. She has decided to undergo further training to support her new marketing experience, and is studying for the Chartered Institute of Marketing Advanced Certificate in the evenings. She hopes that this will lead to a permanent job in marketing.

# Useful addresses

**The Arts Council for England**, 14 Great Peter Street, London SW1P 3NQ; 0171 353 0100

**Arts Council of Northern Ireland**, 185 Stranmillis Road, Belfast BT9 5DU; 01232 381591

**Arts Council of Wales**, Holst House, 9 Museum Place, Cardiff CF1 3NX; 01222 394711

**Scottish Arts Council,** 12 Manor Place, Edinburgh EH3 7DD; 0131 226 6051

*Arts Management Weekly*, Rhinegold Publications, 241 Shaftesbury Avenue, London WC2H 8EH 0171 333 1700

**Stage Newspaper Ltd**, 47 Bermondsey Street, London SE1 3XT; 0171 403 1818

# Further reading

The Arts Council publishes a *List of Useful Contacts*, while the AGCAS booklet *Performing Arts and Arts and Administration* gives an excellent introduction to the sector. The AGCAS occupational profiles, *Arts Administrator* and *Community Arts Worker* give you a feeling for how arts administrators spend the day.

# 9 Information management

Ten to fifteen years ago this chapter would have been called 'Librarianship'. The new name reflects not only a growth in techno-speak but the diversification of information sources – and resourcing – in the past decade. Increasingly, the roles of old-fashioned librarians and new-fangled information officers are becoming blurred, although archive work (see below) is still a distinct area in its own right. If you thought that 'librarianship' was a career for people so timid that they prefer to communicate in whispers, you may be in for a surprise.

Everyone in the information sector must have the following attributes:

◆ good communication skills – contrary to the stereotypical image, this is very much a 'people-centred' job;
◆ organisational ability – information has to be orderly so that it can be used, and someone has to maintain it in that way;
◆ intellectual ability – breadth of knowledge, a good memory, and the ability to think your way laterally out of problems are essential;
◆ a willingness to develop IT skills – so much information is stored electronically these days that most users have to be computer-literate to access it, never mind providers.

## Tasks of the librarian/information officer

There are three key areas of activity: acquisition, organisation, and exploitation.

*Acquisition* involves knowing and predicting what your users need, and where it can be found if you do not have it.

*Organisation* involves classifying your materials according to an established system (library systems are like languages – you can not just make one up and expect to be understood); it also means making sure that materials and records of them in the form of catalogues are synchronised. Budgeting and assigning people to tasks are key features of the higher reaches of information management.

*Exploitation* involves developing the best way for users to gain access to the full range of material stored: providing a reference service to help users help themselves; carrying out searches for specialist individual interests; producing promotional displays, new acquisition lists, abstracts, etc; educating users in retrieval skills.

As with any career, the balance of these activities depends very much on the size of the organisation you work for. You are more likely to specialise the bigger the organisation; in a small, specialist library, you might find yourself doing everything except the cleaning. There are self-employment possibilities in the form of consultancy work, but information management is very largely an institutional career.

## Types of employer

### Public libraries and information services

These are run by local authorities and offer a wide range of services. They range from huge metropolitan institutions like the City of Birmingham Public Library to small branch services with only a few thousand titles. There is usually a local HQ for technical services such as IT and acquisitions, but small local initiatives are common in the form of school liaison and community 'outreach' activities.

## National libraries

National libraries keep extensive collections of books, maps, periodicals and supply reference, lending and general research services. Many people who work in them are administrative staff rather than qualified librarians, and the contact with users can be minimal, except in the reading rooms.

## Educational institutions

Only larger *schools* will employ a specialist librarian; otherwise the job is likely to be done by a qualified teacher with remission of time. For this kind of work it is necessary to have some interest in young people's reading habits and not to regard them as spoilers of the perfect tranquillity of your library!

*Further education colleges* usually deliver a wide range of courses to students of widely differing ability. Many of their libraries are now more like resource centres, dependent on electronic materials as much as books. In this new environment of 'student-centred learning', information management and IT skills have acquired particular prominence.

*Higher education (HE)* could not function without its huge collective resource of books, manuscripts, journals, reference sources and – increasingly – CD-ROMs. Librarians in HE may work on a functional basis (ie be responsible for generic tasks such as cataloguing, acquisitions, reader services) or with a specific departmental remit (selecting books for order, liaising with academic staff, dealing with readers' enquiries, organising information programmes). Some people combine both, depending on the institution.

## Special libraries and information services

Many different kinds of organisations need to keep records of sufficient magnitude to merit specialist management: manufacturers, banks, advertising agencies, architects, professional associations, trade unions, research trusts and institutions, government departments, health organisations, charities, and so on. For each of these a relevant first degree is normally essential, while IT and foreign language skills are highly desirable.

## Qualifications and training

It is often assumed that a career in librarianship is impossible without specialist qualifications. This is only true up to a point. Many people begin as library assistants, which involves a variety of routine tasks: checking that new material has arrived from the publisher; adding details to the catalogue; answering simple inquiries; shelving and re-shelving; issuing books to borrowers. It is possible to get a job of this kind with only four GCSEs (including English), although most employers require at least A-levels.

There is a range of pre-graduate qualifications:

◆ City and Guilds 737 Certificate in Library and Information Competences;
◆ BTEC National Certificate of Achievement in Library and Information Work (offered on day release or by correspondence);
◆ NVQs/SVQs in Information and Library Services are also available.

For graduate qualifications, see the UCAS guide. There are around a dozen BA courses in Information Science, and another dozen in Library and Information Management. All are accredited by the Library Association which publishes details of available courses (see the list of useful addresses at the end of this chapter).

The Library Association also publishes details of the 17 one-year postgraduate courses in librarianship, some of which can be taken part time or by distance learning. You have to bear in mind, however, that competition for places on these courses is quite stiff, so it is necessary to gain a year's practical experience as a library assistant first. Assuming that you get a job after completing your postgraduate work, it is usual to become a member of the Library Association within a year of starting your first appointment. The Institute of Information Scientists accepts new members after five years' experience and a qualification from one of the 15 one-year postgraduate courses which it accredits (again, see the list of useful addresses for this chapter).

# Archive work

Archives are collective memories, consciously produced and maintained by organisations for business or cultural purposes. They may be lodged in banks or country houses; they may consist of photographs or computer disks. The majority of archivists work for the government, but museums, charities and the Church are also major employers. Archivists' work can be surprisingly sociable: about 50 per cent of the time spent, for example, in a County Records Office will be in answering questions relating to family, commercial or topographical history.

Archivists have to evaluate the worth of different kinds of material, deciding what should be kept. They also have to know how to arrange materials so that they are accessible, which involves cataloguing, indexing, and other such careful labour. Conservation is also an important part of their work, since for some of the time they may be handling very old documents and books which have to be stored and used in such a way as to guarantee their survival. There is a public dimension to archive work as well: mounting exhibitions and liaising with schools can be important features of the job, requiring good presentational and interpersonal skills.

Archivists need many of the same skills as librarians, but there are key differences:

◆ archivists are more likely to work on their own, perhaps in unpleasant conditions;
◆ they are more likely to travel away from the archive to evaluate new findings or donations, for example of papers from a company or prominent family;
◆ practical conservation skills are more important than in a library;
◆ knowledge of other languages (modern and ancient, for obvious reasons) is also more desirable because some documents may be indecipherable without it;
◆ physical strength is more important! There may be quite a lot of old boxes to shift.

*Training* possibilities are largely confined to one-year postgraduate courses in archive work. See the AGCAS survey of courses in Heritage Management and Museum Services. As with the equivalent courses in librarianship, it is usually necessary to gain relevant work experience first. Look in your local library for a copy of *Record Repositories in Great Britain* (HMSO), and write to your nearest records office to ask about voluntary work experience. Archival courses are competitive: in addition to your work experience you will almost certainly need an upper second class degree and an early application.

---

## Top Tips

### for Getting into Information Management

◆ As usual, improve your IT skills!

◆ Try to get some voluntary experience in a library, archive or information office of some kind (tourist information booth, box office, ticket office, etc).

◆ If you can't do the above, try anywhere that involves dealing directly with members of the public, such as a shop – this will help to demonstrate that you have the right interpersonal skills.

◆ Contact the Library Association (see Useful addresses at the end of this chapter) for a copy of their *Record: Vacancies Supplement*, and ask about their in-house recruitment agency.

◆ Ask the Library Association about its Graduate Training Opportunities Scheme, which co-ordinates one-year placements for graduate trainees offered (largely) by academic employers.

◆ Write to the Department for Education and Employment to ask about its bursary scheme, which will fund a limited number of places on library and information science courses.

◆ Be prepared to move around to get your first job and to keep moving thereafter in order to gain the right range and depth of experience.

## Case Study

**Emma** graduated in English in 1992. She had come to college with the idea of eventually becoming a librarian, having already worked in a library on Saturdays when she was in the sixth form. In spite of having made this decision, she decided to keep her options open by following a non-vocational degree course rather than one in librarianship. She felt she was good at organising things and she liked working with people. When she graduated she took a graduate trainee post at an HE college. During that time she experienced most aspects of library work, and at the end of the year she applied successfully for a postgraduate library course at a university in the north-west. For this course she was fortunate enough to receive a DfEE bursary. She completed an enjoyable but demanding year only to find that there was no work suited to someone with her qualifications; she didn't really want to go back to being a library assistant if she could help it. So, she took a bold step. She volunteered for a Christian organisation in Ghana. Her brief was to work for six months on a subsistence basis to restore and build up a library which had been neglected for the past eight years. When she arrived, she found herself in a largely oral culture where records were psychological rather than physical. The shelves and cupboards in her workplace were full, not of books, but of toys, agricultural equipment and old saucepans. She had to learn to work without materials she had taken for granted before, and she also had to train someone locally to take over the management of the library when she returned to the UK.

When she came back, fitter and more determined than ever, she applied for about 30 jobs. She was set against working in London, so it took a long time for something to come up. After three months, she got a job as an assistant librarian in a Midlands college of further education with a total student roll of nearly 12,000. At the end of her first year she submitted a 6,000-word professional development report to the Library Association and so became a chartered librarian.

Emma feels that her current job is interesting but not quite ideal. The size of the operation is daunting, and she would like to work in a smaller school library (public library funding is, she feels, a little unpredictable at the moment). At the FE college, the users are staff and students, and the stock is mostly non-fiction. Everything is geared to the courses that are run at the college. She enjoys dealing with students and finding out the answers to obscure problems, and it is good to have to keep pace with IT developments. Although she can see that library services are becoming more technical, she believes there will always be a need for staff to help users in a friendly and informative way.

Emma recommends anyone who is interested in this area as a career to find out what it's really like by getting voluntary experience. 'Don't assume that it's all reading books,' she says, 'because that doesn't really come into it at all!' She adds that if you are applying for a post-graduate course in librarianship or information management, apply for them all – leave nothing to chance in this competitive business.

## Useful addresses

**(Association for Information Management) ASLIB**, 20–24 Old Street, London EC1V 0AP; 0171 253 4488

**Institute of Information Scientists**, 44 Museum Street, London WC1A 1LY; 0171 831 8003

**The Library Association**, 7 Ridgmount Street, London WC1E 7AE; 0171 636 7543

**Royal Commission on Historical Manuscripts**, Quality House, Quality Court, Chancery Lane, London WC2A 1HP; 0171 242 1198

**Records Management Society**, c/o Mrs H. Farley, 6 Sheraton Drive, High Wycombe, Buckinghamshire HP13 6DE; 01494 525040

**The Scottish Record Office**, HM General Register House, Edinburgh EH1 3YY; 0113 5351314

**Society of Archivists**, Information House, 20–24 Old Street, London EC1V 0AP; 0171 253 5087

# Further reading

Careers booklets and leaflets can be obtained from all of the above. The Institute of Information Scientists' list is particularly recommended, as is the Society of Archivists' *Archives as a Career*. In addition, look at the AGCAS booklet, *Information Management and Social Research*. AGCAS also publishes a list of courses in library work and information management. For more information about the routine of different information jobs, try the following AGCAS occupational profiles: *Careers Information Officer, Information Officer, Information Scientist; Librarian, Academic; Librarian, Public.*

# 10 Marketing

Marketing is easier to recognise than to define. The Chartered Institute of Marketing describes it as a 'management process responsible for identifying, anticipating and satisfying customer requirements profitably'. If this sounds like an ambitious and elusive task, it is: marketing entails difficult, well-informed decisions about product development, planning and design, pricing, packaging, sales, advertising, public relations, advertising, distribution and after-sales service. Although some of these functions are performed by specialists, they are all co-ordinated by the marketing one – the need to attain the right 'marketing mix'. This is true whatever the sector – consumer marketing of domestic products, industrial marketing (selling to other manufacturers or suppliers), service marketing of areas such as finance or leisure, or export marketing. Overall, marketeers aim to establish what consumers want, while those in sales try to make sure that consumers actually buy what is aimed at them.

Everyone in marketing needs these qualities:

◆ an enquiring mind – the key question is what motivates consumers;
◆ the ability to work on a variety of products, irrespective of their intrinsic interest ('it's not the product, it's the way you market it', as anyone in the business will tell you);
◆ the drive to solve problems through sound analysis and sound strategy;
◆ the ability to work in a team and get on with other people – marketing is very much a collective enterprise;

◆ good numeracy – marketeers deal with figures a lot of the time;

◆ good communication skills – this means not only the confidence to give presentations and write persuasively, but the ability to listen and understand an opposing point of view. Remember that all marketeers are devoted to understanding what other people want!

## The jobs

There are three main levels of job:

1. Marketing manager.
2. Product/brand manager (this means having responsibility for one particular product: making sure that everything is right under all the headings listed below).
3. Marketing assistant (this involves a variety of tasks such as organising exhibitions, writing brochures or prospectuses, updating information on databases, and so on. The clerical nature of this work demands good writing and computer skills).

Naturally, most people start at the bottom. Tasks to be co-ordinated or completed at all three levels include the following.

*Market research*, or deciding what information is needed about an area of the market, how to get it, and how to analyse it constructively.

*Product development*, or working with design and production departments to advise on amendments based on consumer feedback.

*Pricing*, or establishing what the market and production costs demand for the price of each item.

*Sales and distribution*, or the analysis of where something has sold, in what quantities, and in response to what specific advertising initiatives.

*Promotion*, or working with advertisers, design consultants, direct marketing organisations and public relations agents to establish the right profile for the product in the media and the environment at large.

*Export marketing,* or liaising with local agents in the target countries to advise on strategy, perhaps bearing in mind linguistic, cultural or political differences.

Whatever the level or area you are in, marketing is not (contrary to the popular image) a particularly glamorous business: careful planning, monitoring and following through are its essence. Remember, too, that marketing is potentially quite stressful. One bad miscalculation could cost jobs.

---

### Top Tips

## for Getting into Marketing

Although there are a number of qualifications available in marketing, they are largely intended for people already in work. This means that employers will be looking for personal qualities and experience rather than a specific body of knowledge. So, you should aim to explore the following areas.

◆ Get some work experience in a consumer environment and develop a sense of what sells and why.

◆ Do your own case study of one area of the market by finding out which companies are involved, what their target groups are, and how successfully they sell their products to those groups.

◆ Write speculative applications and follow them up with a phone call – marketing requires personal determination and the drive to succeed.

◆ Look at the Top Tips in the next two chapters of this book.

◆ Consider the range of postgraduate courses listed in the AGCAS survey of postgraduate courses in marketing, advertising and public relations.

◆ Look for openings in the following magazines: *Marketing, Marketing Week, Campaign, The Grocer.* Monday's *Guardian* and Wednesday's *Independent* and *Daily Telegraph* contain advertisements for higher profile vacancies, while your local and regional papers should be consulted for work closer to home.

---

## Case Study

**Nick** had A-levels in English and sociology when he went to work in the customer liaison department of a large engineering company. His job was interesting but always, in his words, 'reactive'. He wanted to be part of the main driving force behind the company's obvious success, and soon found out that that force was to be found in the marketing department.

To his dismay he discovered that marketing only recruited graduates. He didn't want to take three years out to get a degree, so he started talking to the people in marketing about what they did and how they did it. When they had to work late or meet very tight deadlines, he offered to help them out. He also found some books about marketing in the public library ('dull as dishwater, but some of it helped') and began to read the *Financial Times* to get a picture of what was going on in other companies. Eventually a vacancy came up in the firm for a marketing specialist with the responsibility of supporting product managers on key products.

After he'd been given the job his new boss told him that one of the reasons he had been successful, in spite of the graduate-only policy, was that he had intuitively used marketing techniques to get the job. He had discovered a market he wanted to enter; researched it thoroughly through contacts and background reading; tested the market by helping people out when they were busy; and completed his launch by getting a strong application together.

He has now acquired some autonomy in making decisions about key areas such as pricing, promotion design and management, and customer liaison, at home and overseas. He enjoys the responsibility and the feeling of being able to take credit for success, but there are frustrations. In particular, he thinks that marketing doesn't enjoy as high a profile as it should and that people in other areas of the company with different priorities regard him and his colleagues as cosmetic. The result is that there are constant battles over new initiatives and deadlines. Overall, however, Nick sees marketing as a rewarding job which allows you to develop 'both the analytical and creative sides of your brain'. He says that 'there is no such thing as a typical day', but he generally works from nine until six, with half an hour for lunch, and divides his time between meetings (internal and external), planning, writing, telephoning, harrying colleagues for information or material, and checking reports. There's plenty of variety, he adds, but it can be very hectic. He's had to learn to organise his time to the last minute.

## Useful addresses

**Chartered Institute of Marketing**, Moor Hall, Cookham, Berkshire SL6 9QH; 01628 427500. (Booklets and booklists available, plus details of qualifications.)

**The Communications, Advertising and Marketing Foundation (CAM)**, Abford House, 15 Wilton Road, London SW1V 1NJ; 0171 8287506. (Booklets available.)

## Further reading

See the AGCAS booklet, *Marketing and Market Research*. The AGCAS occupational profiles for *Marketing Assistant: Consumer; Marketing Assistant: Industrial; Marketing: Brand Manager* are all enlightening. N Hart and N Waite's Kogan Page title of 1994, *How to Get On in Marketing*, is also useful.

The addresses of the standard trade journals are as follows.
*Marketing*, Haymarket Business Publications, 30 Lancaster Gate, London W2 3BR
*Campaign*, Haymarket Publishing Group, 174 Hammersmith Road, London W6 7JP
*Marketing Week*, Centaur Communications Ltd, St Giles House, 50 Poland Street, London W1V 4AX
*The Grocer*, William Reed Publishing Ltd, Broadfield Park, Crawley, West Sussex RH11 9RT

# Sales

There are significant overlaps between this area of employment and those explained in previous chapters, especially advertising, publishing and marketing. In many ways, indeed, sales is seen as the poor relation of those other, more glamorous industries, as a job tainted with dishonest persuasion. This is pure snobbery. It goes without question that any product, however well designed in itself, needs to be sold effectively if it is to be a success; and sales is such a dynamic and transferable sector that it demands space of its own. No economy could prosper without a supply of good salespeople.

Sales people rely on a body of skills:

◆ excellent communication skills – you do not have to be blessed with an oracular silver spoon, but you do need to be confident, persuasive, and be able to cope with resistance or even hostility;

◆ negotiating skills – you have to be able to think quickly in response to a potential customer's stated needs or views without selling your employer short;

◆ good personal organisation – sales representatives usually plan their own days to ensure that they get through everything to schedule; in addition, they often work from home;

◆ the ability to absorb and recall under pressure a considerable amount of information about what they are selling;

◆ perseverance and a pretty thick skin to cope with those who turn out not to be the most enthusiastic buyers (what would you reply if a shop owner turned around and said, 'Look, I run this place and I'm telling you that I don't want any'?).

# The jobs

*Sales managers* manage the team of sales staff by setting objectives, maintaining training programmes, chairing sales meetings, monitoring performance and generally motivating people.

*Sales representatives* are the front-line troops, dealing with store managers or buyers, and trying to meet the targets set by management. Personal sales obviously have an impact on company profitability; poor performance, by the same token, leaves the individual representative exposed.

Under those two broad umbrellas, people work in a variety of settings, including *export sales*, for which a second language and background cultural knowledge are very useful; *consumer sales*, which tends to involve selling fast-moving consumer goods to retailers and wholesalers, and working within a specific region to establish and maintain targets. Then there are *technical and medical sales*, where, to be honest, people with science qualifications have more chance; *media space sales*, or selling advertising space in newspapers or journals to individuals or organisations; and *telesales*, which is often maligned, but can lead to visiting prospective customers and giving presentations – a good way in to more secure and interesting work; or *financial sales*, which means selling loans, mortgages and other financial services either for an organisation such as a bank or independently (knowledge of consumer protection legislation is essential in this area). Finally, there is the area of *sales administration*, or support for the sales team through record-keeping and briefing.

# Training

There is very little outside the in-service training offered by many employers in product knowledge and sales techniques, although there are graduate sales and recruitment agencies (see useful addresses, below). The Institute of Sales and Marketing Management (again, see useful addresses), offers a number of correspondence courses, although prior experience is desirable and sometimes necessary for these.

---

## Top Tips

# for Getting into Sales

The tips for sales are very similar to those for marketing. In addition to all the market research recommended to you on page 68, try getting involved in a college or school role-play society to try out your confidence and manoeuvrability under pressure. Also, improve your second language or start to acquire one fast.

---

## Case Study

**Nick** graduated with a degree in English and Drama. He spent a little while 'getting used to the outside world', earning money in a succession of short-term jobs, and finally settled on a career in sales. He had been active in student politics and felt that the personal confidence which this gave him could be exploited to the full in his chosen career. He also acknowledged the value of the presentational and time management skills he had developed during his undergraduate course.

Nick applied by CV to a graduate sales recruitment and training agency and was invited to their assessment day. He enjoyed the whole selection process, which was tough but not daunting, and after a month's training with the agency was taken on by a small chemical manufacturing company in the Midlands.

Now he spends four days of the week on the road, visiting a variety of existing and potential customers, all of them requiring silicon and polyurethane. The range is considerable: his clients make pottery, armaments, engineering hardware and other products. His day is a mixture of appointments and casual calls at an average of eight per day. Sometimes he talks to the managing director in the boardroom, sometimes to the purchasing officer over a cup of tea. He observes that 'there are a lot of nice people out there' but admits to having one or two awkward customers on his books. Planning each day is time consuming and painstaking. He allows 20 or so minutes for each appointment and about half an hour's travelling time in between.

The day doesn't end with his last appointment, however. At the end of each working day he has to send action request forms back to head office, who in turn send out information and sales quotations to the customers he has visited. And that fifth day when he's not on the road? He's in the office, planning the following week, booking appointments and following up leads.

Nick says that it is almost like being self-employed. He needs a lot of self-discipline but at the same time he is under pressure to meet the sales targets set by his field manager (who, incidentally, was out on the road with him for the first few months of his job). The company he works for is small, with only 14 employees, but it is typical of the kind of organisation many graduates will work for. It is an expanding firm, however, with European ambitions, and Nick hopes that his knowledge of Italian may be called on. The job is pressurised, but the rewards are quite good, and Nick has complete faith in the oldest sales adage of all: 'Most customers buy the salesman first, and the product second'.

---

# Useful addresses

**The Institute of Sales and Marketing Management (ISMM)**, National Westminster House, 31 Upper George Street, Luton, Bedfordshire, LU1 2RD

**Managing and Marketing Sales Association (MAMSA)**, New House, School Lane, Warmingham, Sandbach, Cheshire, CW11 0GD

# Further reading

MAMSA can supply details of training and recruitment agencies, while ISMM can send you *Your Career in Selling and Sales Management*. In addition to the AGCAS booklet, *Sales and Purchasing*, see another Kogan Page title, N Hart and N Waite's *How to Get On in Marketing*. Hobson's publish a *Marketing, Retailing and Sales Casebook*. The Institute of Export (address in Chapter 12) publishes a useful information pack, while the following AGCAS occupational profiles give you a strong flavour of life in sales: *Media Sales Executive; Sales Executive: Consumer; Sales Executive: Export; Sales Executive: Medical; Sales Executive: Publishing; Sales Executive: Technical; Sales Executive: Advertising.*

# 12 Management and administration

You may remember from Table 1.2 in Chapter 1 that 18.7 per cent of first destinations for English graduates are in 'management and administration'. As the University of London's guide to careers in management puts it, 'there's a lot of it about'. People in management jobs are often the first to wonder whether anyone else in the world does 'real' work (in case you haven't noticed). Now it is time to ask exactly what those 18.7 per cent are getting up to.

Managers are, indeed, everywhere: in the commercial sector, in the civil service, in the armed forces, in prisons, schools, colleges and universities. In some professions, such as teaching, social work or nursing, it is necessary to build up expertise before moving into management. Whatever the sector, all managers are responsible for

- ◆ organising tasks and people;
- ◆ delegating functions to others in the team;
- ◆ making key decisions;
- ◆ taking necessary risks;
- ◆ making sure that outcomes are achieved;
- ◆ managing constant personal pressure on themselves;
- ◆ getting the best out of the people under them.

They do all these things in an environment of unending change, which, as the industrial giant Unilever once said, is the only constant in the business world.

The term 'administration' overlaps significantly with 'management'; many posts which used to be called 'administrative' are now described as 'managerial', especially in public sector organisations such as the civil service, local government and the health service. Equally, the line between public and private sector administration is no longer as clear as it once was, given new imperatives of productivity and accountability. All administrators need to be able to do two key things:

1.  Understand the complex sets of conventions and procedures which underpin their work – administration is in important respects the opposite of invention, and administrators are there to make the existing system function effectively rather than change it radically;
2.  Be able to brief other people, whether users or bosses, in those procedures so that they grasp them fully – such briefing may be personal or directed towards the work of a committee.

These two functions demand a range of skills: personal organisation; coolness when faced with a deadline; teamwork; good written and oral communication skills; the drive to make things work properly; sensitivity to other people's views and backgrounds; the ability to think logically; good numeracy; a certain amount of commercial nous; and the ability to handle the broad concepts which supply the rationale for everything to which the organisation is committed.

---

## Case Study

**Lucy** graduated in English four years ago. In her final year she had visited her college careers centre and taken a computerised interest guide which suggested that she might work in the retail industry. She read the literature and was attracted by the range of opportunities it offered. As a former secretary of the student union entertainments committee, she knew she had the capacity to organise events successfully.

Her first job came as the result of a speculative application. She had written to a local department store to ask about graduate recruitment, and they responded by sending her some information and an application form. She was placed on the store's management training scheme and worked in a number of different departments in order to gain an overall view of the business. Now she is assistant manager of the perfumery department, with responsibility for 25 full- and part-time employees. It is the biggest section in the store, so Lucy is in a good position to apply for the post of full departmental manager when it arises. Buying manager is another possibility.

She shares with her manager the responsibility for training her staff, ensuring that correct procedures are followed, for security, customer service, stock balancing, and dealing with sales representatives. Her main satisfaction is in 'getting people to do their jobs well' and in seeing sales figures increasing because of their efforts. Above all, she enjoys working with so many different people and getting to know their individual qualities. Her English degree was especially useful for this job, she says, because of the presentation skills it taught her, because it enabled her to write in a direct, concise way, and because it developed her self-confidence. She adds that her degree fostered a key quality of 'inquisitiveness' – the need to know what's going on behind the scenes, why certain products sell and others don't, why person x isn't taking to her work as well as person y, why certain managerial decisions are taken.

---

# Types of employer

*Local government* is a major employer of administrative staff, with many different branches of work: trading standards, housing, leisure and recreation, careers guidance, social work, accountancy, libraries and information, and others. All these are open to people with English qualifications, and all can involve promotion to managerial level following suitable training and experience. There are opportunities to enter as an administrative trainee, but recruitment is likely to be *ad hoc* rather than through the kind of regular programme undertaken by the Civil Service.

*The National Health Service* is the UK's largest employer, and until recently was Europe's largest. It runs a graduate general management scheme at the national level, as well as regional schemes in finance and personnel management. Some hospitals or units will recruit directly.

*Higher and further education* establishments employ a significant bureaucracy to work on publicity, student admissions, planning, committees, school liaison, accommodation, estates, quality assurance, and a huge range of other tasks. Recruitment is occasional and advertised either through the national supplements (*The Times*

*Educational* and *Higher Educational*, Tuesday's *Guardian*) or in local newspapers. Administrative opportunities also exist in other education-related bodies such as funding councils, research councils and trusts and examination boards.

*The Civil Service* employs nearly 120,000 people in 'managerial' positions covering a wide range of areas including ministries, prisons, tax offices and customs and excise centres. Civil Service culture has changed over the past few years: it is no longer a job for life, while pay increments have been replaced by performance-related bonuses. Commercial criteria and practices are much more in evidence than before. There is still the 'Fast Stream Development Programme' which takes in about 150 graduates each year in policy development schemes, while the emphasis on graduate qualifications is increasing, with BAs and BScs now taking up approximately 65 per cent of those jobs previously offered to people with A-level qualifications only.

## Training

Larger companies have traditionally recruited to specialist training schemes in which recent graduates spend up to two years working in different jobs (sometimes in widely different locations) and possibly acquiring extra qualifications by distance learning. Middle and top management jobs are usually filled by people who have been through such schemes. Consult your HE careers service for details. The following directories are invaluable: *Prospects Today; Prospects Finalist; GO;* and *GET*.

Graduate training schemes are numerous, but there are, nonetheless, signs of change. More employers now recruit directly to a specific job, side-stepping dedicated training programmes which are expensive to run and entail long-term costs which finances might not be able to bear; in addition, they can result in successful trainees simply being poached by other employers. Such developments place a great onus on the young graduate to do everything possible to get prepared by other means.

### Top Tips

## for Getting into Management and Administration

You will have noticed from the list of skills demanded by management and administration jobs that many of the qualities you need to be able to show can be gained partly within your academic curriculum but also, to a significant extent, outside it. Hence the advice offered below.

◆ Aim to develop your communication skills by getting involved in student committee work – staff/student liaison groups and student societies are two good instances.

◆ Try to land some part-time or voluntary work which involves organising something and motivating other people to get involved.

◆ When you have the opportunity to get involved in academic work which entails group presentations, take it. Some English students shy away from such activity because they believe it undermines the personal element in their studies, whereas in fact it strengthens your overall profile immeasurably.

◆ Aim to develop leadership skills by volunteering to be an officer in a student society, and embrace any responsibility offered you in part-time or summer work.

◆ If your school or college offers an 'Insight into Management' course, sign up for it; the same goes for any 'Young Enterprise' schemes.

◆ Look out for vacation employment schemes which may be run by local companies – your careers service or Training and Enterprise Council should have details. Supermarkets, local government and the Civil Service all have short-term placement schemes.

◆ Consider the possibility of a postgraduate qualification (full or part-time) in management – there is a complete list of such courses in the

AGCAS survey of postgraduate courses. There is no guarantee of work following such a course, but it would put you in touch with a number of professional practitioners and other key contacts.

◆ Be prepared to take a lower level post than you might ultimately want, to give yourself some experience of office work and business life in general. This will leave you very well placed to apply for a management training scheme, and will get your foot in the proverbial door for organisations which recruit internally for senior positions.

Now for some case studies. Because Management and Administration is such a diverse area, there are two quite different studies here, one in the private sector and one in the public sector.

---

## Case Study

**Catherine** works as a practice administrator for a GP in the north of England. She graduated five years ago with a degree in English and spent three years working as an interviewer for a market research company. During this time, she improved her IT skills by attending a basic City and Guilds computing course at her local college of further education.

One day she saw an advertisement in the local paper for a graduate to work in a GP surgery, initially loading information on to the computer system, but with the possibility of promotion to an administrative post. It was a large practice, with two sites, six doctors, 25 other staff and over 12,000 patients. She got the job. After gaining initial experience of the computer system and administrative procedures, Catherine was given the task of setting up an office system which would enable the doctors to claim fees from the NHS for different services they provided, whether immunising children or screening women for breast cancer. The system had to be easy to use and maintain, involving the doctors themselves in a minimum of work beyond what their patients required of them. As with all user-friendly systems, setting it up was a complex task. She now has to ensure that all data are entered by the doctors in a standard form via their own personal computers; potential target groups of patients are contacted so that revenue is maintained and increased (this involves supervising other members of staff in writing letters and making telephone calls); an audit trail is clearly established so that records are transparent to external scrutiny; doctors new to the practice are familiar with its procedures; and that all staff follow the correct procedures and maintain strict confidentiality in dealing with patients' records.

She says that the essence of the job is 'making sure that things run smoothly and that people are doing the right things by communicating what it is that needs to be done'. She cites organisational skills as the most important ones which she brought to her job and developed in it. Her IT skills were instrumental in getting her the job, but an ability to sort through a mountain of paperwork and give priority to what is important is also crucial. On reflection, she thinks that the research skills she learned during her degree were the most valuable in what she does now: sorting through masses of printed information, deciding what to include and in what order. She adds that her job is very similar to many administrative posts in the public sector, but she gets satisfaction from making sure that health care is delivered to patients as effectively as the system will allow.

---

## Case Study

**Joe** graduated over ten years ago with a degree in English from a college of higher education. He had had a great time as an undergraduate, and been a member of the football team. He had always had holiday jobs, and found that when he looked for work full time potential employers always valued his 'team outlook'. He knew he wanted to be in the sort of job where he could make decisions, so he looked for management trainee posts. Finally, he was offered a job with a manufacturer, which sold parts to garages.

The company had been running its management trainee programme for several years, and it was fairly typical of such schemes. Joe spent his first six months in a warehouse shadowing people with managerial responsibility; he served on the trade counter, went out with the sales force, delivered parts to garages, worked in the administrative office, and learned about accounting procedures. The idea was to learn about every aspect of the organisation and to meet people from all its different levels. At the end of the scheme he was given a 12-month job in the south coast branch as a buyer. After that he continued to build up his knowledge by working as a salesman for two years, calling on garages and developing working relationships with owners and staff. His reward came two years later, when he was appointed branch manager with responsibility for a dozen staff and a turnover of one million pounds. Senior management thought, however, that that one million should be two or more, and Joe's challenge was to turn the branch around. A challenge it certainly was: he had to introduce new procedures, identify members of staff in need of additional training, and sack some others.

Having met and come through the challenge, Joe now works in a branch with a long record of success and he has to maintain that good record. He hopes that within the next two years he will move on to be manager of one of the largest depots in the organisation. In Joe's view, 'Managing people can be the most rewarding but also the most frustrating job. Follow the adage that since you have two ears and one mouth, you should use use them in that ratio.' He numbers among his satisfactions 'a good quality of life' and the 'buzz when things go well'. The main challenge is to get everyone working towards the same goals willingly, but he does tend to take it personally when things don't quite go the way he wants.

And his degree-level experience? What has being an English graduate got to do with managing a car parts depot? He says that it trained him to expect more than one side to any problem, and to keep asking questions.

---

## Useful addresses

For public sector training opportunities, write to:

**The Careers Information Office**, Local Government Management Board, Arndale House, The Arndale Centre, Luton, Bedfordshire LU1 2TS; 01582 451166

**Graduate and Schools Liaison Branch**, Cabinet Office, Office of Public Service, Horse Guards Road, London SW1P 3AL; 0171 270 5034

**The NHS Executive**, Management Training Scheme, Room GN3, Quarry House, Quarry Hill, Leeds LS2 7UE; 0113 2546139

**Northern Ireland Regional Development Unit**, Central Services Agency, 25–27 Adelaide Street, Belfast BT2 8FH; 01232 324431

Recruitment Manager, Programmes Team, **NHS Staff College Wales**, Hensol Castle, Pontyclun, Mid Glamorgan CF72 8YS; 01792 703011/703008

**Scottish Health Service Management Development Group**, Scottish Health Service Centre, Crewe Road South, Edinburgh EH4 2LF; 0131 3322335

The following professional bodies offer information about training opportunities in the private sector:

**Chartered Institute of Management Accountants**, 63 Portland Place, London W1N 4AB

**Institute of Administrative Management**, 40 Chatsworth Parade, Petts Wood, Orpington, Kent BRS 1RW

**Institute of Charity Fundraising Managers**, Market Towers, 1 Nine Elms Lane, London SW8 5NQ

**Institute of Export**, Export House, 64 Clifton Street, London EC2A 4HB

**Institute of Housing**, Octavia House, Westwood Business Park, Westwood Way, Coventry CV4 8JP

**Institute of Industrial Managers**, Rochester House, 66 Little Ealing Lane, London W5 4XX

**Institute of Management Consultants**, 32/33 Hatton Garden, London EC1N 8DL

**Institute of Management Services**, 1 Cecil Court, London Road, Enfield EN2 6DD

**Institute of Personnel Management**, IPM House, 35 Camp Road, Wimbledon, London SW19 4UX

not forgetting

**Institute of Purchasing and Supply**, Easton House, Church Street, Easton on the Hill, Stamford, Lincolnshire PE9 3NZ

**Management Consultancies Association**, 11 West Halkin Street, London SW1X 8JL

**Women in Management**, 64 Marryat Road, Wimbledon, London SW19 5BN

# Further reading

For the Civil Service (including addresses of departments recruiting people to administrative/managerial posts) see the following HMSO publications: *The Civil Service Yearbook, Executive Officer, The Civil Service Today and Tomorrow, Finding your Way around Whitehall and beyond.* You can also find out information on the Internet at: http://www.open.gov.uk/co/fsaesd/fsaed.htm

For the Health service, see *The NHS Yearbook* (Highgrove Publishing, 1996/7), *Directory of Hospitals and NHS Trusts* (Longman, 1996), *The NHS Handbook* (Macmillan, 1995).

For local government, see *CATLOG: Careers and Training in Local Government* (Hobson, 1996) and *Municipal Yearbook* (Newman Books, 1996/7).

The AGCAS booklets, *Administration and Public Sector Management, Personnel Work* and *Office Management and Secretarial Services* are also very useful, while the Careers and Occupations Information Centre (COIC) job outlines, *The Civil Service (no 52), The Diplomatic Service (no. 28), Local Government Administration (no. 46)* and *Personnel Work (no. 20),* should also be consulted. Pitman's *Guide to Business Schools* and Hobson's *Graduate Studies* give details of postgraduate courses in administration and management. The University of London Careers Advisory Service's *Careers in Management* is an excellent guide. For more information about the day-to-day demands of different administrative/managerial jobs, try the following AGCAS occupational profiles: *Administrator, Local Government; Civil Service Administrator; GCHQ Executive Officer; GCHQ Graduate Trainee; Manager, Health Service; Administrator, Higher Education.*

# 13 The future of English for employment

We saw in the introductory chapters that academics' views of the value of English differ markedly from those of employers. The question of the future of the subject depends likewise on where your desk is. Academics will talk about the future of English in terms of the challenges of modularity, the increasing diversity of critical and theoretical approaches, the erosion of long-held notions of a fixed canon of inherently 'great' works of literature. For employers, the focus is more likely to be on whether English graduates can bring a core of reliable competences and attributes to the workplace, and whether they can genuinely demonstrate the independence and flexibility of thinking so prized in many a university and college mission statement.

Whether those two sets of questions can be reconciled is a question for another book, although it has been argued, for example, that:

a) modular schemes encourage – at least in principle – greater flexibility in the learning of different competences, as well as a more disciplined approach to deadlines and time management in general, and

b) the increasingly non-elitist nature of English studies, together with the fresh grounding in historical contexts which it has recently cultivated, make it less antipathetic to worldly considerations than it often was in its more pastoral days.

Such arguments are controversial, but you should have worked out by now that if you want determinate answers, English is probably not the subject for you!

There are, nonetheless, developments afoot which appear likely to affect the future provision of English as an academic subject in ways distinct enough for the most ardent empiricist. This book was written just as the results of two important inquiries were emerging. Their convergence of emphasis is striking, and suggests a future pattern for the relationship between English Studies and the employment market. If there is one term which summarises the similarities between the report of the Dearing Inquiry into Higher Education (July 1997) and that of Higher Education Quality Council's 'Graduate Standards Programme' (November 1996), it is 'explicitness': explicitness about what is to be achieved in a given course, why it is to be achieved, whether it has been achieved, and for whom its achievement is beneficial.

Such explicitness does not announce the imminent collapse of non-vocational courses, but a refusal – very much in line with what this book has had to say about English and the employment market – to accept a long-standing differentiation between the vocational and the non-vocational. In English Studies it will mean more conscious and systematic attention to the skills set out in Chapter 2 of this book, as well as the parallel pursuit of specific competences in languages, information technology, and other potential passports to employment. Many degrees in English already bear such characteristics: in addition to the study of canonical and marginalised authors, or theories of language and culture, there may be components in word-processing, Japanese and counselling.

Erosion of the old distinction will not only be achieved by scattering pragmatic components around the edges of intellectual courses. There will be a heightened emphasis on fostering the application of 'knowledge and understanding' for the 'benefit of the economy and society'. To a large extent, that must mean addressing explicitly the qualities which knowledge and understanding bring. Both Dearing and the HEQC inquiry went to great lengths to seek the views of employers, whose views of the desirable qualities of graduates included the following:

- communication
- application of number
- problem-solving
- working with others
- improving one's own learning and performance
- having learned how to learn.

Notice that these are largely attributes rather than specific competences. We are back where we began: with the proven capacity of English to nurture *approaches* to work which seem unexpectedly well-fitted to the needs of the marketplace. Great changes in the education system may be upon us, but there is every likelihood that English will continue as the popular subject it has always been for the best of pragmatic and intellectual reasons.

# 14 Careers information on the Internet

Here is a selection of useful web addresses. New sites conveying new information are being developed all the time. Many of the professional organisations mentioned in this book have their own sites which display careers information and offer insight into the industry concerned. Other sites, such as Datalake, give details of specific vacancies. Consult your nearest careers advisory service for further details.

## *Publishing*

**Periodical Publishers Association**
http://www/ppa.co.uk

**Publishers Association**
http://www.publishers.org.uk

## *Advertising*

**Advertising Association**
http://www.adassoc.org.uk

**Institute of Practitioners in Advertising**
http://www.mark.ipa.co.uk

## Teaching

### Teacher Training Agency
http://www.teach.org.uk

## *TEFL*

### Trinity College
http://www.trinitycollege.co.uk

### British Council
http://www.britcoun.org.uk

## *Marketing*

### Institute of Marketing
http://www.im.co.uk

### Institute of Export
http://www.export.co.uk

## *Management*

### Civil Service
http://www.open.gov.uk

### Civil Service fast track recruitment
http://www.rasnet.co.uk

### METRA
http://www.datalake.com.lgo

For details of management trainee vacancies:

### Datalake
http://www.datalake.com/home.html

### CSU
http://www.man.ac.uk

## Information management

### Library Association
http://www.la-hq.org.uk
orhttp://www.la-rvs.org.uk

## Arts administration

### Arts Council
http://www.artscouncil.org.uk

## Journalism

### Newspaper Society
http://www.newspapersoc.org.uk

### NCTJ
http://www.itecharlow.co.uk /nctj/

### Periodicals Training Council
http://www.ppa.co.uk

### Reuters
http://www.reuters.com

### ITN
http://www.itn.co.uk

### BBC
http://www.bbc.co.uk /jobs/uk

# Index